CLARIDGE'S

THE
COCKTAIL
BOOK

CLARIDGE'S

THE
COCKTAIL
BOOK

PHOTOGRAPHY BY JOHN CAREY

ILLUSTRATIONS BY CLYM EVERNDEN

RESEARCH & EDITING BY
DENIS BROCI & NATHAN MCCARLEY-O'NEILL

MITCHELL BEAZLEY

Contents

Introduction

What makes a Claridge's cocktail? Is it the finest of ingredients, the mastery of the mixologist, the way it is served – with a flourish – in delicate, bespoke glassware? Or is it the sublime setting: dashing waiters impeccably dressed in bow ties and crushed velvet, and lights dimmed so you never have to wonder if it's too early for a glass of something? As with any good cocktail, there is an alchemy that creates an elusive magic that is more than the sum of its parts.

There is a certain swagger to an evening that begins at a Claridge's bar. Gauntlet down, it declares that tonight we celebrate – even if it's just the mere fact that such an extraordinary place still exists. In the inimitable words of our artist in residence David Downton, 'Claridge's is Claridge's and everywhere else is everywhere else'.

Here you will find echoes of London's glorious past: tables where shipping magnates have written deals directly on linen tablecloths (and later received a bill for the cleaning), rooms where the Bright Young Things drank daiquiris, dazzled and danced. Where Marlene Dietrich checked in for weeks at a time, entertaining a succession of lovers who would reportedly leave at dawn. Photographs of Churchill, Audrey Hepburn and Jackie O – all former patrons – gaze down upon you, fireplaces blaze and there is a sense that, just at this moment, perfectly crafted drink in hand, you are precisely where you are meant to be.

When happily ensconced in the intimate embrace of The Fumoir or the butter-soft leather banquettes of Claridge's Bar, it is easy to see why the hotel – and its perfectly mixed drinks – have become something of a refuge for the great and the good over the years (or indeed the beautiful and the damned – the theme of Kate Moss's thirtieth birthday, held here in 2004). Perfectly poured drinks have played a starring role in the hotel's history. Run by the Mivart family as a guesthouse in 1812, the original hotel on Brook Street often welcomed the Prince Regent and his companions, as well as – rather glamorously – expelled international royals determined to live out their exile in style.

Following a change of ownership to William and Marianne Claridge in 1854, the hotel's reputation soared to new heights thanks to a royal visit from Empress Eugénie of France, wife of Napoleon III, in 1860. She received Queen Victoria and gave the hotel a royal seal of approval. Reportedly partial to a combination of Scotch malt whisky and claret, her Majesty Queen Victoria was something of a trailblazer on our capital's cocktail scene.

The turn of the century saw Londoners develop a burgeoning thirst for American 'mixed drinks', blending two or more spirits with bitters and sugar. Cocktails had gained popularity across the pond in the latter half of the 19th century, before Prohibition ensured their inevitable status, and London saw a host of American bars opening in response. Those mixed drinks were surely present when ownership of the hotel passed to English theatrical impresario and hotelier Richard D'Oyly Carte in 1893. More importantly — after a complete redesign of the building by CW Stephens — they were there when the hotel reopened to great fanfare in 1898 (and were likely the cause of the 'generous time' mentioned in newspaper reports of the reopening).

It was at this point that another female trailblazer set the cocktail world alight. Ada Coleman was hired to work in the Claridge's flower shop (a kindness extended by D'Oyly Carte after the death of Coleman's father). She quickly befriended the hotel's wine butler, and he, finding an unusually receptive audience, showed the young florist how to mix a cocktail; a Manhattan, according to a 1926 interview.

Coleman quickly developed a flair for delivering perfectly mixed drinks and perfectly timed wit in equal measure. She was soon offered a job at The Savoy's American Bar, making her one of just 150 female bartenders worldwide and as renowned as any of her celebrity clientele. While there, she invented — for actor Sir Charles Hawtrey — the Hanky Panky cocktail, a drink we still serve today (see page 58). She rose to become head bartender and, by the time of her retirement in 1926, was one of the world's best-known bartenders.

While the classics on the menu would be instantly recognizable to Coleman, cocktails at Claridge's have also changed to reflect the times. Honorary drinks were created for Queen Elizabeth's Coronation in 1953. During USSR prime minister Nikita Khrushchev and Communist Party secretary Nikolai Bulganin's controversial stay in 1956, the Soviet politicians held a cocktail party in the Royal Suite, said to be so crowded that 'buttons popped off jackets and wine was spilled on ladies' dresses'. Movie stars and royalty, from Cary Grant to Princess Margaret, Alfred Hitchcock to Audrey Hepburn, stepped into the Foyer for an aperitif or two before taking dinner at the Claridge's Grill, later christened The Causerie.

Today, there are no fewer than four bars within this grand hotel, led by the Claridge's Bar itself. Designed by the late David Collins as a soft-focus sanctuary, the bar has its own entrance through a heavy velvet curtain and discreet door on to Davies Street. The orders, like the interiors, are classic and elegant: Laurent-Perrier La Cuvée NV Champagne in chilled panelled flutes, classic Champagne cocktails and intricate snacks in elegant silverware. Sitting on a garnet-red leather barstool, a guest can soak in the theatre of the mixology while savouring a pre-dinner aperitif such as the Flapper: the signature crème de cassis-spiked Champagne cocktail created for the bar's launch in 1998 (see page 24).

Across the famous chequered hallway, behind an original Lalique door panel and tucked away like a jewellery box, you will find The Fumoir. This intimate, Art Deco bar takes cues from the 1920s, with original Basil Ionides mirrors, low lighting, a marble horseshoe bar and delicious Prohibition-era cocktails – such as the Brandy Crusta and White Lady (see pages 134 and 115) – that explain why the decade roared. Portraits by William Klein gaze moodily from deep claret-hued walls, while soft velvet seats arranged in close quarters beckon you to stay awhile longer. It is said that time is meaningless in The Fumoir. As Downton – who is often to be found at his unofficial office of table 4 – notes, 'In The Fumoir, noon can feel like midnight and midnight can stretch until noon.'

Just next door but a world away is the bar at Davies and Brook, the Michelin-starred restaurant overseen by Daniel Humm of New York's three-starred Eleven Madison Park. Here, cocktails are the gateway to a gastronomic, kitchen-inspired experience: everything from sous-vide-infused spirits to milk-washed fruit punches.

Last but not least of the Claridge's bars is the most recently founded: The Painter's Room, inspired by murals that hung there in the 1930s when it was called 'The Painted Room'. Taking inspiration from the era and paying tribute

to the iconic Art Deco Claridge's doors, this bar is an awakening feast for the senses, with colourful artwork by Annie Morris, sumptuous leather stools and a menu inspired by the culture, art and design of Europe. Ingredients are at the core of the creative process here – all deeply considered, with excess ingredients left behind, to result in drinks with flavours in their purest, simplest form. Saint Remy (see page 76) is a variation on the Martini, with apple and quince, and inspired by Van Gogh's *Almond Blossom*.

Together, this formidable quartet serve almost 36,000 cocktails every year. Each is produced by a bartender both fastidiously trained and singularly focused on preserving the excellence for which the hotel is known and loved. Within this book are more than 400 cocktail recipes, spanning many decades and the circumference of the globe.

Over the course of the hotel's history, menus have evolved and adapted to reflect changing tastes, with the classics proving resilient, and Claridge's, ever at the forefront of evolution, is now placed to lead the way for the cocktail making generation of the future. Through each iteration and innovation, one thing has remained constant: when one is drinking a cocktail at Claridge's, nothing else in the world matters.

Boat Race Eve Ball

18 Mars 1932

CLARIDGE'S

THE CAUSERIE ★ CLARIDGE'S

Claridge's Cocktails · Coronation Year

A long Refreshing Cooler - 5/6
Playing Fields - - - 5/6

Cocktails
Salutation - - 5/0   The Comet - - 5/6
Wedding Bells - 5/0   Banjino - - - 5/0
Windsor Rose - 5/6   Reverie - - - 5/0
Iolanthe - - - 5/6

GE'S

CLARIDGE'S

CLARIDGE'S

Claridge's

Tuesday, 24th May 1932

BANQUETING
WINE LIST

A SPECIAL CLARIDGES COCKTAIL

WEDDING BELLS

CLARIDGE'S

Claridge's
Wine
List

LIST OF PRICES

COCKTAILS		s. d.	MIXED DRINKS	Per
Bronx	... ...	4 6	Gin and Lime ...	
Banjino	...	4 6	Gin and Orange Squash	
Five Rings	...	5 0	Gin and Orange Bitters	
Happy Medium	...	5 0	Rum and Lime	
Lilliput	...	4 6	Gin and French	
Martini	...	4 6	Gin and Italian	
Manhattan	...	5 0	Pink Gin	
Old Fashioned	...	5 0		
Sloe Measure	...	5 6	**SPIRITS**	
Side Car	...	4 6	Brandy	
Tudor Rose	...	5 0	Liqueur Scot	
White Lady	...	5 0	Scotch and	
Wedding Bells	...	5 0	Gin and	

FIZZES
Savoy Hotel Special
Gin ...
Pimms No. 1

SOURS
Savoy Hotel Specia
Gin ...
Whisky
Brandy

COOLERS
Long Tom Colli

HIGHBALLS
Whisky, Bran

MINERALS
Ginger Ale
Ginger Bee
Soda

JA. 49

A NEW CLARIDGE'S COCKTAIL

LE CHANTECLAIR

IN HONOUR
OF THE STATE VISIT OF
THE PRESIDENT OF FRANCE
and
MADAME AURIOL

Claridge's

e National
Historic Interest o

CLARID
London

Claridge's

CLARIDGE'S
LONDON

TAIL MENU

17th Feb

Claridge's cocktails by numbers

HOW MANY COCKTAILS DO WE MAKE?

53,714

PER ANNUM

WHICH IS THE MOST POPULAR COCKTAIL?

The Flapper

SEE PAGE 24

HOW MANY MARTINIS DO WE POUR?

13,604

PER ANNUM, MOST POURED STRAIGHT
FROM THE FREEZER AT -19°C (-2°F)

WHICH ARE THE MOST POPULAR BAR SNACKS?

Tempura Prawns

1,786 PER ANNUM, OR 16,074 PRAWNS FOR
THIS DISH ALONE AND...

Duck Rolls

14,148 PER ANNUM

HOW MANY GLASSES OF CHAMPAGNE DO WE SERVE?

35,425

PER ANNUM

HOW MANY CHAMPAGNE COCKTAILS DO WE MAKE?

9,552

PER ANNUM

HOW MANY CITRUS FRUITS (LEMON, LIME, ORANGE AND GRAPEFRUIT) DO WE USE?

234,539

PER ANNUM

WHAT IS THE MOST EXPENSIVE COCKTAIL WE HAVE EVER SOLD?

Many guests like to order signature drinks made with specific premium brands. The most expensive was a £1,000 Old Fashioned, made with Gibson's Rye Whisky 1905, a special bottling for the Pendennis Club in Louisville, Kentucky.

← William Wallace (see page 46)

Creating the perfect bar at home

THE BAR ITSELF

The very dedicated may wish to build a home bar, but a well-stocked drinks cabinet or trolley will more than suffice. Cocktails are all about the theatre, so try to position your station where you entertain most. Here we have listed the essentials, but you may wish to add more as you hone your skills.

GLASSWARE

From julep tins and cognac glasses to gossamer-thin Champagne flutes, an expanding collection of glassware is common among mixologists. In addition to presentation, the cocktail glass plays a vital role in the bibulous experience, altering both the aroma and taste of any given drink. While there are infinite options available – and we very much encourage you to start your own collection – you need a minimum of four types of glass for this book:

- flute – for serving drinks containing Champagne

- rocks – for short drinks poured over cubed, crushed or block ice

- highball – for tall drinks poured over cubed or crushed ice

- coupe – for short drinks served without ice

All glassware should be chilled before use. This is particularly important for coupes, as the drinks served in these are not typically prepared with ice.

Equipment

To paraphrase William Morris, one must own nothing that you do not know to be useful or believe to be beautiful. Happily, all of the below hit the spot on both counts and will help you create professional standard cocktails *à la maison*. Always remember to sterilize your equipment before use.

BOSTON SHAKER TINS

This pair of tin shakers slot together, creating a perfect seal that allows for vigorous mixing. A good size set should have ample room for two drinks to be shaken with a generous helping of ice cubes. A weighted version is recommended, as it allows the bartender to get a better grip.

COBBLER / THREE-PIECE SHAKER

This three-piece shaker, with an inbuilt strainer, is usually slightly smaller in volume and size: 350–500ml (12–18fl oz), compared to the Boston (700ml/ 1¼ pint). The best cobbler shakers come in polished stainless steel.

MIXING GLASS/TIN

Essential for stirred drinks, a mixing glass or tin allows a bartender to combine a cocktail gently without diluting it – and to interact and share an anecdote or two while the alchemy occurs. Glass versions can be beautiful and are less expensive than their stainless-steel counterparts. However, the latter are less breakable and chill drinks faster.

STRAINER

This circular metal utensil, with tightly wound coils, prevents anything uninvited appearing in your cocktail. At Claridge's, a Hawthorne strainer is typically used – this fits just inside a Boston shaker tin. The coiled spring is designed to hold back the ice. However, a bartender can 'open the gate' (move the strainer back slightly) to allow slivers of ice into the drink if desired. Claridge's bartenders usually strain a second time, using a fine strainer.

FINE STRAINER

This is a small, steel mesh basket, such as you might use to steep loose-leaf tea. Used with the Hawthorne strainer, it ensures drinks have a smooth and refined texture. This is especially useful when crafting a cocktail using egg whites.

JIGGERS

This measuring tool is used for every Claridge's cocktail, except the Claridge's Martini, which is free-poured. At the hotel, a Japanese-style jigger is preferred as it has multiple etchings inside indicating different measurements, allowing for greater accuracy. Hold the jigger straight when adding liquor and pour right to the top of the line.

BAR SPOON

This long, slender spoon reaches to the bottom of the tallest mixing glass. At Claridge's, you will find 40cm (16in) teardrop bar spoons with an elegant spiral finish and a thin shaft, to allow fingers to grip and rotate with ease. There is an art to stirring: movement should come from the wrist, not the elbow, fingers should be wrapped around the spoon so they move together, and there should be almost no noise against the glass. Claridge's bartenders are trained to stir using both hands, so they can create multiple drinks at the same time.

ICE PICK AND KNIFE

An ice pick and knife can add a touch of drama to your cocktail-making. They are, naturally, very sharp and should be treated carefully, lest your cocktail party end in more drama than planned. Hold the pick firmly and keep one finger near the sharp edge. This allows you to connect accurately with the ice.

MUDDLER

The bartender's answer to a pestle and mortar, a muddler lightly crushes fruits, peels and herbs together. This releases their juices, oils and aromas.

ATOMIZER

Essential for a proper Martini, this simple spritzing device allows you to 'season' the glass with a mist that completes a drink.

ICE TONGS

These can be things of beauty and make for the perfect finishing touch to your mixing. Use them to add or remove ice cubes from glasses and shakers. They are also useful for adjusting garnishes.

Techniques

BUILD

As with cooking, the order of ingredients affects the outcome. As a general rule, you should build your cocktail in the following order:

- volatile ingredients – bitters, absinthe, saline or citric solutions
- sweeteners – sugar, syrups, cordials, shrubs
- juice
- liqueur/sherry/fortified wine
- base spirit
- egg white – if you are making a sour or a flip, add the egg after the other ingredients (but before the ice), as otherwise it can begin to 'cook' in the citrus and alcohol.
- ice – unless otherwise instructed in a recipe, you should add ice only once all the ingredients, excluding anything sparkling, are combined.
- anything sparkling, such as Champagne or soda. This is to prevent it going flat.

SHAKE

In mixology, shaking has a fourfold effect: mixing, chilling, diluting and adding texture. It is usually reserved for particularly robust drinks containing citrus, juice or sugar, which need a little help to integrate.

Start by building ingredients in the smaller of the shaker tins. Add ice up to the rim, then lock the larger tin over the top, at an angle. This creates a vacuum, holding the tins together.

Give the top of the shaker a firm tap to make sure it is secure. Hold firmly, with one hand on each tin, and shake vigorously. The ice should vibrate and rotate around the shaker, rather than simply move up and down.

How long to shake is a matter of taste and opinion. Under-shaking can stop the mixture diluting properly. This can result in an overly acidic flavour if you are using citrus fruits, or an overly strong drink. Over-shaking can dilute the blend too much, creating a flat or underwhelming result. Find your ideal by experimenting.

A sour containing egg white will need extra shaking for integration and aeration. A drink with a spice, such as the Penicillin (see page 100), requires a harder shake, so there is adequate dilution to prevent a harsh taste. A lighter drink, such as the Osaka Punch (see page 138), needs a shorter shake, so the flavours don't get lost. Some cocktails, such as the Silver Beet (see page 132), require dry shaking – without ice – before shaking *with* ice, so the ingredients have a chance to meet before they are diluted. Finally, a shaken drink served over crushed ice – such as a piña colada (see page 158) – benefits from a 'whip shake': a fast, short shake with two or three small pieces of ice. This chills the drink rapidly, without adding too much water.

STIR

Stirring cocktails involves ice cubes and a bar spoon, to cool and gently dilute the drink. The more ice used, and the faster it is moved, the quicker the cocktail cools. As with shaking, there is no precise time to stir: it is a question of environment – the temperature of the room, the ingredients, the equipment – and personal taste. And, as with shaking, there is an equilibrium to stirring. Too little results in strong, overpowering cocktails. Too much runs a risk of watering down the aromas. It is simply a matter of practice.

As a general rule, when stirring drinks served over ice, such as a negroni or Old Fashioned, err on the side of under-stirring, because the ice will continue to melt in the glass. Martinis, Manhattans and other drinks served 'straight up' (without ice) can benefit from a longer stir until they reach an ambient temperature.

For all cocktails, shaken or stirred, keep your equipment and glassware in the refrigerator (or freezer, along with gin or vodka, in the case of a Martini). Handle the mixing glass as little as possible, to keep it cool.

STRAIN

For a smooth finish, strain after shaking or stirring. Sit a Hawthorne strainer atop the shaker tin or mixing glass. Hold in place while you pour

Garnishes

the cocktail into the serving glass. Perfectionists may wish to double-strain: hold a fine mesh tea strainer over the serving glass as you pour through the Hawthorne, so the drink passes through both.

To create syrups, shrubs, cordials, infusions and some cocktails, you will need to strain through a paper coffee filter. Always make sure to pre-soak the coffee filter in water before using, to remove any aromas.

MUDDLE

The trick to muddling – pressing fruits and herbs together – is to gently press and twist simultaneously. Don't press too hard: this can fragment the ingredients and cause bitter flavours.

FLOAT

This technique allows a bartender to create layered cocktails. Hold a bar spoon upside down over the top of the cocktail. Rest the tip of the spoon on the inner edge of the glass, so that it sits just above the top layer of the cocktail. Slowly and carefully, pour the final ingredient over the back of the spoon so that the liquid floats on the top of the cocktail. This will create a distinct layer. As a rule of thumb, the more sugar in an ingredient, the better it will float.

CHURN

To churn is to stir ingredients at high speed, with crushed ice. This quickly chills them.

Whether it's a subtle spray of citrus oils from an Amalfi lemon twist or a salty green olive in a bath of dry vermouth and gin, a garnish adds a key final flourish. It bonds the flavours and aromas while adding a pleasing visual note. Not to be skipped.

COIN AND TWIST

Adding a vibrant pop of colour, citrus fruit zest also contains inviting aromatic oils that can provide a delicious fragrance and finish. A sharp paring knife is needed.

For a coin, use the knife to remove a neat circle of zest, avoiding the fruit. Hold the coin over the cocktail, zest side facing the glass. Squeeze lightly to spritz oils over the surface of the drink, then run the squeezed zest along the rim of the glass. Place the coin into the drink, peel side up.

For a twist, use the knife to remove a long, thin strip of zest. Trim it with the knife, then use your fingers to curl it into a twist and place it in the glass.

DISCARD

Sometimes, aromatic oils from the zest are desired but, for aesthetic reasons, the peel itself is not. Pinch a coin of citrus zest over the cocktail, zest side facing the glass, and express the juices and oils over the cocktail. Before throwing away the zest, rub it around the rim of the glass for an extra dash of citrus flavour.

RIM

This simple technique adds a professional touch to any drink. Begin by pouring the salt (or whatever ingredient you would like, it could be freeze dried raspberry powder, cacao powder or sugar) on to a plate. Rub a lemon slice around the rim of the chilled serving glass. Then, holding the serving glass by its side, gently roll the outside rim of the glass in the salt. Lightly tap off the excess. Neaten with a cocktail stick. (To half-rim a glass, follow the same method but only rub the lemon round half the rim before coating with salt.)

Products
& ingredients

Techniques and equipment are important, but ingredients are the real heroes of the cocktail hour.

Below is a list of the spirits you will find most useful when establishing a home bar, along with some of the hotel's favoured brands.

The brands chosen in these recipes reflect what guests at Claridge's enjoy, but you are of course welcome to use any that you wish. When substituting a different brand, it may be necessary to adjust the measurements to balance the recipe or simply add a dash of bitters or sugar to taste.

- **vodka**
  Claridge's favourites: *Belvedere, Grey Goose, Ketel One*

- **gin**
  Claridge's favourites: *Tanqueray, Plymouth, Hepple, Boatyard*

- **tequila and mezcal**
  Claridge's favourites: *Ocho, Tapatio, Ilegal*

- **rum**
  Claridge's favourites: *Bacardí Heritage, Havana Club 3 Year, El Dorado 15 Year*

- **Scotch whisky**
  Claridge's favourites: *Johnnie Walker Black Label, Chivas, Laphroaig 10 Year*

- **Irish whiskey**
  Claridge's favourites: *Green Spot, Redbreast 12 Year*

- **American whiskey**
  Claridge's favourites: *Michter's Bourbon, Michter's Rye*

- **Japanese whisky**
  Claridge's favourites: *Suntory Chita, Suntory Toki*

- **Cognac**
  Claridge's favourites: *Hennessy VSOP, Merlet Brothers Blend*

- **liqueurs**
  Claridge's favourites: *Mr Black Coffee Liqueur, Merlet Triple Sec, St-Germain elderflower liqueur*

- **vermouth**
  Claridge's favourites: *Dolin Dry, Martini Rosso*

- **bitters**
  Claridge's favourites: *Campari, Aperol, Angostura bitters, orange bitters, Peychaud's bitters*

- **sodas**
  Claridge's favourites: *Fever-Tree* sodas and tonics, *Three Cents Pink Grapefruit Soda*, *Fentimans Ginger Ale*, *London Essence Company* soda collection

- **syrup**
  Claridge's favourites: *Bristol Syrup Company's* simple sugar syrup, orgeat syrup and coconut syrup. *Monin's* range of syrups is also readily available, or you can simply make your own (see below).

Sugar Syrup

MAKES 500ML (18FL OZ)

250g (9oz) caster sugar
250ml (9fl oz) water

Combine the sugar and measured water in a saucepan over a low to medium heat and stir until the sugar has dissolved (do not let the mixture boil).

Leave to cool before pouring into an airtight bottle. This will keep in the refrigerator for up to 4 weeks.

A NOTE ON ICE

Please do not embark on cocktail-making without plentiful ice to hand. It is both an essential ingredient and a critical piece of equipment. Where possible – and we understand that sometimes needs must – use the correct ice for the cocktail. This ensures that the drink reaches your guest in the perfect condition and that the ice lasts as long as required.

Ice cubes are for shaken and stirred cocktails, and for long drinks.

Ice blocks are for drinks that require little to no dilution, such as a negroni. A drink served over an ice block will hold its flavour longer than one served over cubes or crushed ice.

Crushed ice is for strong-flavoured drinks containing fruit and spices.

A NOTE ON MEASUREMENTS

Before you begin preparations for the cocktail hour, it is essential that you consider your equipment. Are the measures in metric? If so, you're set. If not, beware! The bartenders at Claridge's always use metric (rather than imperial) measurements for the greatest accuracy. All the cocktails in this book were created and tested in metric, so we kindly insist that you also use metric measurements when reproducing our recipes.

If your preference is imperial measurements, these have been provided. But please note that the resultant cocktails may differ slightly from the originals therefore.

Champagne

&

Sparkling

← Alfonso (see page 36)

The Roaring City

MAKES 1 DRINK

25ml (1fl oz) Curry Leaf-infused
    Mancino Secco Vermouth (see
    page 203)
25ml (1fl oz) Pineapple Tepache (see
    page 215)
10ml (¼fl oz) sugar syrup (see page 21)
50ml (2fl oz) Laurent-Perrier La
    Cuvée NV Champagne
Curry leaf, to garnish

Build the ingredients in a chilled
rocks glass over an ice block, then
stir. Garnish with a curry leaf.

✦ Credit: Miriam Schofield, MO Bar,
Singapore

The Flapper

MAKES 1 DRINK

15ml (½fl oz) Briottet Crème de Cassis
15ml (½fl oz) Boiron strawberry purée
Laurent-Perrier La Cuvée NV
    Champagne, to top up
½ a strawberry, to garnish

In a cocktail shaker, stir the crème
de cassis and strawberry purée
together, then fine-strain into a flute.
Top up with the Champagne and
garnish with half a strawberry on the
rim of the glass.

✦ Created for the opening of Claridge's Bar
in 1998

Harmony Royale

MAKES 1 DRINK

20ml (¾fl oz) Rémy Martin VSOP
    Cognac
10ml (¼fl oz) Maraschino
15ml (½fl oz) sugar syrup (see page 21)
10ml (¼fl oz) lemon juice
1 strawberry
Laurent-Perrier La Cuvée NV
    Champagne, to top up

In a cocktail shaker, shake all the
ingredients, except the Champagne,
with ice cubes, then fine-strain into a
flute. Top up with the Champagne.

Rouge 75

MAKES 1 DRINK

25ml (1fl oz) Plymouth Sloe Gin
15ml (½fl oz) sugar syrup (see page 21)
10ml (¼fl oz) lemon juice
Laurent-Perrier Rosé NV Champagne,
    to top up
Orange coin, to garnish

In a cocktail shaker, shake all the
ingredients, except the Champagne,
with ice cubes, then fine-strain into
a flute. Top up with the Champagne.
Express the orange coin over the top,
then discard.

Bellini

MAKES 1 DRINK

30ml (1fl oz) Boiron white peach purée
145ml (5fl oz) Laurent-Perrier La
    Cuvée NV Champagne

Build the white peach purée and
Champagne in a mixing glass and
then pour slowly into a flute.

→ The Flapper

Summer Cup

MAKES 1 DRINK

4 blackberries
2 lemon slices
20ml (¾fl oz) Rémy Martin VSOP
      Cognac
20ml (¾fl oz) Graham's Late Bottled
      Vintage Port
10ml (¼fl oz) Merlet Crème de Mûre
5ml (1 tsp) sugar syrup (see page 21)
2 dashes of orange bitters
Laurent-Perrier La Cuvée NV
      Champagne, to top up
2 orange slices, to garnish
Cinnamon stick, to garnish

Muddle the blackberries and lemon
slices in a cocktail shaker, then add
the remaining ingredients, except
the Champagne, and churn with
crushed ice. Pour into a chilled large
rocks glass and top up with the
Champagne and more crushed ice.
Garnish with the orange slices and a
cinnamon stick.

✦ Adapted by: Oliver Blackburn,
Claridge's Bar, London

Beauty of Season

MAKES 1 DRINK

25ml (1fl oz) Ki No Bi Gin
20ml (¾fl oz) Italicus Rosolio Di
      Bergamotto
20ml (¾fl oz) lemon juice
20ml (¾fl oz) Winter Syrup (see
      page 197)
1 egg white
Perrier-Jouët Grand Brut NV, to
      top up

In a cocktail shaker, dry shake all the
ingredients, except the Champagne,
then add ice cubes and shake again.
Fine-strain into a chilled coupe. Top
up with the Champagne.

✦ Credit: Denis Broci, Claridge's Bar,
London

Negroni Sbagliato

MAKES 1 DRINK

25ml (1fl oz) Martini Rosso
25ml (1fl oz) Campari
Laurent-Perrier La Cuvée NV
      Champagne, to top up
Orange slice, to garnish

Build the Martini and Campari in a
chilled rocks glass over an ice block.
Top up with the Champagne and stir
gently. Garnish with a slice of orange.

✦ Credit: Mirko Stocchetto, Bar Basso,
Milan

All Year Round

MAKES 1 DRINK

3 fresh pineapple chunks, plus a
      pineapple wedge, to garnish
30ml (1fl oz) Barsol Pisco
25ml (1fl oz) John D Taylor's Velvet
      Falernum
20ml (¾fl oz) lemon juice
Laurent-Perrier La Cuvée NV
      Champagne, to top up

Muddle the pineapple chunks in
a cocktail shaker, then add the
remaining ingredients, except the
Champagne, and shake well with ice
cubes. Fine-strain into a flute and
top up with the Champagne. Garnish
with a wedge of pineapple on the rim
of the glass.

✦ Credit: Filippo Ricci, Claridge's Bar,
London

Death in Venice

MAKES 1 DRINK

15ml (½fl oz) Campari
2 dashes of Bitter Truth Grapefruit
      Bitters
Laurent-Perrier La Cuvée NV
      Champagne, to top up
Orange coin, to garnish

Build the ingredients in a flute and
stir gently. Express the orange coin
over the top, then discard.

✦ Credit: Tony Conigliaro, 69 Colebrooke
Row, London

→ Beauty of Season

French 75

MAKES 1 DRINK

25ml (1fl oz) Plymouth Gin
10ml (¼fl oz) lemon juice
15ml (½fl oz) sugar syrup (see page 21)
Laurent-Perrier La Cuvée NV
    Champagne, to top up
Lemon twist, to garnish

In a cocktail shaker, shake all the ingredients, except the Champagne, with ice cubes, then fine-strain into a flute. Top up with the Champagne and garnish with a lemon twist.

✦ **Credit: Harry MacElhone,** *ABC of Mixing Cocktails* **(1923)**

Pineapple Twinkle

MAKES 1 DRINK

15ml (½fl oz) Belvedere Vodka
15ml (½fl oz) St-Germain elderflower
    liqueur
15ml (½fl oz) Toasted Pineapple Syrup
    (see page 195)
20ml (¾fl oz) lemon juice
Laurent-Perrier La Cuvée NV
    Champagne, to top up

In a cocktail shaker, shake all the ingredients, except the Champagne, with ice cubes, then fine-strain into a flute. Top up with the Champagne.

✦ **Credit: Elon Soddu, The Savoy, London**

Champagne Cocktail

MAKES 1 DRINK

1 white sugar cube
2 dashes of Angostura bitters
25ml (1fl oz) Martell Cordon Bleu
    Cognac
Laurent-Perrier La Cuvée NV
    Champagne, to top up
Orange coin, to garnish

Place the sugar cube in a flute and soak with the Angostura bitters. Add the Cognac, then top up with the Champagne and stir. Express the orange coin over the top, then discard.

Russian Spring Punch

MAKES 1 DRINK

25ml (1fl oz) Ketel One Vodka
10ml (¼fl oz) Merlet Crème de Cassis
15ml (½fl oz) lemon juice
15ml (½fl oz) sugar syrup (see page 21)
Laurent-Perrier La Cuvée NV
    Champagne, to top up
Lemon wedge, to garnish
Raspberry, to garnish

In a cocktail shaker, shake all the ingredients, except the Champagne, with ice cubes, then fine-strain into a chilled highball filled with ice cubes. Top up with the Champagne and garnish with a lemon wedge and a raspberry.

✦ **Credit: Dick Bradsell, Zanzibar, London**

Death in the Afternoon

MAKES 1 DRINK

15ml (½fl oz) Pernod Absinthe
5ml (1 tsp) sugar syrup (see page 21)
Laurent-Perrier La Cuvée NV
    Champagne, to top up
Orange and lemon coins, to garnish

Build the absinthe and sugar syrup into a mixing glass over ice cubes and stir gently. Strain into a flute and top up with the Champagne. Express the orange and lemon coins over the top, then discard.

✦ **Credit: Ernest Hemingway, Paris**

Cucumbagne

MAKES 1 DRINK

**2 cucumber slices, plus a ribbon of
    cucumber, to garnish**
20ml (¾fl oz) Hendrick's Gin
10ml (¼fl oz) lime juice
10ml (¼fl oz) sugar syrup (see page 21)
**Laurent-Perrier La Cuvée NV
    Champagne, to top up**

Muddle the cucumber slices in
a cocktail shaker, then add the
remaining ingredients, except the
Champagne, and shake well with ice
cubes. Fine-strain into a flute. Top
up with the Champagne and garnish
with a cucumber ribbon.

✦ Credit: Jorge Oliveira, Claridge's Bar,
London

Hand in Hand

MAKES 1 DRINK

**30ml (1fl oz) Olive-infused Martini
    Ambrato (see page 205)**
15ml (½fl oz) OP Anderson Aquavit
**10ml (¼fl oz) Olive Leaf Cordial (see
    page 192)**
5ml (1 tsp) Æcorn Aperitif Dry
25ml (1fl oz) Fever-Tree Soda Water
**25ml (1fl oz) Laurent-Perrier Rosé NV
    Champagne**
Olive, to garnish

Build the ingredients, except the
soda water and the Champagne, in
a chilled goblet, then add ice cubes
and give a little stir. Top up with the
soda water and Champagne and
garnish with an olive.

✦ Credit: Kaitlin Wilkes, Blue Bar,
The Berkeley, London

Champagne Colada

MAKES 1 DRINK

**10ml (¼fl oz) Bacardí Ron Superior
    Heritage Limited Edition**
**10ml (¼fl oz) Bacardí Carta Blanca
    Rum**
5ml (1 tsp) Trois Rivières Blanc Rhum
40ml (1½fl oz) pineapple juice
**35ml (1fl oz) Pineapple Cordial (see
    page 192)**
3 scoops of coconut sorbet
**50ml (1fl oz) Laurent-Perrier La Cuvée
    NV Champagne**
Raw coconut chips, to garnish

Blend all the ingredients with 20ml
(¾fl oz) of the Champagne and
half a scoop of crushed ice until
silky smooth. Pour the remaining
Champagne into a colada glass, add
the blended cocktail and garnish
with coconut chips.

✦ Credit: Chris Moore, Coupette, London

Bucks Fizz

MAKES 1 DRINK

50ml (2fl oz) orange juice
5ml (1 tsp) Grand Marnier
**50ml (2fl oz) Laurent-Perrier La
    Cuvée NV Champagne**

Build the ingredients in a mixing
glass and then pour slowly into a
flute.

Homage

MAKES 1 DRINK

1 dash of Pernod Absinthe
7.5ml (1½ tsp) RinQuinQuin à la Pêche
7.5ml (1½ tsp) Campari
**160ml (5½fl oz) Billecart-Salmon
    Champagne Brut Rosé**

Stir all the ingredients, except the
Champagne, in a mixing glass with
ice cubes for 8 to 10 rotations. Strain
into a flute and top up with the
Champagne.

✦ Credit: Nathan McCarley-O'Neill,
The Painter's Room, London

J'adore

MAKES 1 DRINK

10ml (¼fl oz) Ketel One Vodka
15ml (½fl oz) Briottet Manzana Verde
15ml (½fl oz) Capreolus Perry Pear
    Eau de Vie
10ml (¼fl oz) lemon juice
10ml (¼fl oz) sugar syrup (see page 21)
5ml (1 tsp) Bristol Syrup Company
    Raspberry
1 dash of Pernod Absinthe
Laurent-Perrier La Cuvée NV
    Champagne, to top up
Raspberry, to garnish

In a cocktail shaker, shake all the
ingredients, except the Champagne,
with ice cubes, then fine-strain into
a flute. Top up with the Champagne
and garnish with a raspberry.

✦ Credit: Daniel Baernreuther, Claridge's
Bar, London

Great Maiden's Blush

MAKES 1 DRINK

25ml (1fl oz) Tanqueray London Dry
    Gin
25ml (1fl oz) Belvoir Elderflower
    Cordial
25ml (1fl oz) lemon juice
2 dashes of Fee Brothers Rhubarb
    Bitters
Laurent-Perrier Rosé NV Champagne,
    to top up
Pink grapefruit slice, to garnish

Build the ingredients, except the
Champagne, in a chilled wine glass.
Top up with ice cubes and the
Champagne, then stir. Garnish with
a slice of pink grapefruit.

✦ Credit: Denis Broci, Claridge's Bar,
London

La Dolce Vita

MAKES 1 DRINK

30ml (1fl oz) Italicus Rosolio Di
    Bergamotto
15ml (½fl oz) Mandarin Napoléon
10ml (¼fl oz) yuzu juice
2 dashes of Fee Brothers Rhubarb
    Bitters
35ml (1fl oz) Laurent-Perrier Rosé NV
    Champagne
Lemon twist, to garnish

Build all the ingredients, except
the Champagne, in a mixing glass
with ice cubes and stir. Strain into a
chilled coupe and top up with the
Champagne. Garnish with a lemon
twist.

✦ Credit: Luigi Gallo, Davies and Brook,
London

Old Cuban

MAKES 1 DRINK

25ml (1fl oz) Havana Club 7 Year Old
    Rum
10ml (¼fl oz) lime juice
15ml (½fl oz) sugar syrup (see page 21)
2 dashes of Angostura bitters
6 mint leaves
Laurent-Perrier La Cuvée NV
    Champagne, to top up

In a cocktail shaker, shake all the
ingredients, except the Champagne,
with ice cubes, then fine-strain into
a chilled coupe. Top up with the
Champagne.

El Fumadero

Maldon smoked sea salt
20ml (¾fl oz) Tapatio Blanco Tequila
25ml (1fl oz) pink grapefruit juice
15ml (½fl oz) sugar syrup (see page 21)
Laurent-Perrier La Cuvée NV
    Champagne, to top up

Rim a flute with Maldon smoked sea salt (see page 19). In a cocktail shaker, shake all the ingredients, except the Champagne, with ice cubes, then fine-strain into the glass. Top up with the Champagne.

✦ Credit: Riccardo Semeria, The Fumoir, London

Twinkle

20ml (¾fl oz) Ketel One Vodka
15ml (½fl oz) Belvoir Elderflower
    Cordial
Laurent-Perrier La Cuvée NV
    Champagne, to top up
Lemon coin, to garnish

In a cocktail shaker, shake the vodka and cordial with ice cubes, then fine-strain into a chilled coupe. Top up with the Champagne and garnish with a lemon coin.

✦ Credit: Tony Conigliaro, The Lonsdale, London

Moonwalk

25ml (1fl oz) Grand Marnier
20ml (¾fl oz) grapefruit juice
2 dashes of rose water
Laurent-Perrier La Cuvée NV
    Champagne, to top up

In a cocktail shaker, shake all the ingredients, except the Champagne, with ice cubes, then strain into a chilled wine glass. Top up with the Champagne.

✦ Credit: Joe Gilmore, The Savoy, London

Champagne Cobbler

10ml (¼fl oz) Maraschino
15ml (½fl oz) sugar syrup (see page 21)
2 lemon wedges
2 orange wedges, plus 2 extra wedges,
    to garnish
2 fresh pineapple wedges, plus an
    extra wedge, to garnish
Laurent-Perrier La Cuvée NV
    Champagne, to top up
2 raspberries, to garnish
Mint sprig, to garnish

Muddle all the ingredients, except the Champagne, in a cocktail shaker, then shake well with ice cubes. Fine-strain into a short stemmed wine glass, add crushed ice and top up with the Champagne. Garnish with 2 orange wedges, a pineapple wedge, 2 raspberrries and a mint sprig.

Knickerbocker Royale

25ml (1fl oz) Havana Club Especial
    Rum
10ml (¼fl oz) Combier Triple Sec
5ml (1 tsp) lime juice
10ml (¼fl oz) sugar syrup (see page 21)
2 raspberries
Laurent-Perrier La Cuvée NV
    Champagne, to top up

In a cocktail shaker, shake all the ingredients, except the Champagne, with ice cubes, then fine-strain into a flute. Top up with the Champagne.

→ Champagne Cobbler

Le Roi Soleil

MAKES 1 DRINK

1 white sugar cube
2.5ml (½ tsp) Bristol Syrup Company Grenadine
15ml (½fl oz) Campari
10ml (¼fl oz) Mandarin Napoléon
Laurent-Perrier La Cuvée NV Champagne, to top up

Place the sugar cube in a small dish. Pour the grenadine over so that the sugar cube is coated but not soaked. In a cocktail shaker, stir the Campari and Mandarin Napoléon together very briefly, with an ice block to chill but not to dilute, then fine-strain into a flute. Add the grenadine-soaked sugar cube and top up with the Champagne.

✦ Credit: Brian Silva, Home House, London

National #2

MAKES 1 DRINK

35ml (1fl oz) Bacardí Ron Superior Heritage Limited Edition
10ml (¼fl oz) Briottet Crème d'Abricot
15ml (½fl oz) pineapple juice
10ml (¼fl oz) lime juice
15ml (½fl oz) sugar syrup (see page 21)
Laurent-Perrier La Cuvée NV Champagne, to top up

In a cocktail shaker, shake all the ingredients, except the Champagne, with ice cubes, then fine-strain into a flute. Top up with the Champagne.

✦ Credit: Charles H Baker Jr, *The Gentleman's Companion* (1939)

Madame y Patrón

MAKES 1 DRINK

35ml (1fl oz) Patrón Añejo Tequila
20ml (¾fl oz) Lustau Oloroso Sherry
20ml (¾fl oz) Agave Caramel (see page 212)
6 dashes of Xocolatl Mole Bitters
Laurent-Perrier La Cuvée NV Champagne, to top up

Stir all the ingredients, except the Champagne, in a mixing glass with ice cubes, then fine-strain into a chilled coupe. Top up with the Champagne.

✦ Credit: Andrea Melis, Blue Bar, The Berkeley, London

Alfonso

MAKES 1 DRINK

1 white sugar cube
2 dashes of Angostura bitters
20ml (¾fl oz) Dubonnet
Laurent-Perrier La Cuvée NV Champagne, to top up

Place the sugar cube in a flute and soak with the Angostura bitters. Add the Dubonnet, top up with the Champagne and stir.

Apricot Fizz

MAKES 1 DRINK

25ml (1fl oz) Grey Goose L'Orange Vodka
5ml (1tsp) Campari
25ml (1fl oz) Apricot Sorbet (see page 212)
Laurent-Perrier La Cuvée NV Champagne, to top up

Stir all the ingredients, except the Champagne, in a mixing glass and stir. Fine-strain into a flute, and top up with the Champagne.

Third Time Lucky

MAKES 1 DRINK

Freeze dried raspberry Powder
25ml (1fl oz) Martini Riserva Speciale Rubino
25ml (1fl oz) Martini Riserva Speciale Bitter
10ml (¼fl oz) Bombay Sapphire Gin
25ml (1fl oz) Raspberry Shrub (see page 191)
Laurent-Perrier La Cuvée NV Champagne, to top up

Half-rim the outside of a chilled wine glass with freeze dried raspberry powder (see page 19). Build the ingredients, except the Champagne, in the glass, then add a splash of Champagne.

✦ Credit: Gábor Onufer, Claridge's Bar, London

Mojito Royale

MAKES 1 DRINK

40ml (1½fl oz) Havana Club Selección de Maestros Rum
20ml (¾fl oz) Pomelo Sherbet (see page 211)
20ml (¾fl oz) lime juice
5ml (1 tsp) sugar syrup (see page 21)
5 drops of Vango Bitters (see page 213), plus a few extra drops, to garnish
Laurent-Perrier La Cuvée NV Champagne, to top up
Mint sprig, to garnish

Churn all the ingredients, except the Champagne, in a highball with crushed ice. Add more crushed ice as needed and top up with the Champagne. Garnish with the vango bitters and a mint sprig.

✦ Adapted by: Kiril Stefanov, Claridge's Bar, London

Lavandula Daiquiri

MAKES 1 DRINK

50ml (2fl oz) Bacardí Carta Blanca Rum
35ml (1fl oz) lime juice
20ml (¾fl oz) Monin Lavender Syrup
Laurent-Perrier La Cuvée NV Champagne, to top up
Lavender sprig, to garnish

In a cocktail shaker, shake all the ingredients, except the Champagne, with ice cubes, then fine-strain into a chilled coupe. Top up with the Champagne and garnish with a lavender sprig.

✦ Credit: Oliver Blackburn, Claridge's Bar, London

Jimmy Roosevelt

MAKES 1 DRINK

20ml (¾fl oz) Rémy Martin VSOP Cognac
5ml (1 tsp) Green Chartreuse
10ml (¼fl oz) sugar syrup (see page 21)
2 dashes of Angostura bitters
Laurent-Perrier La Cuvée NV Champagne, to top up
Orange coin, to garnish

In a cocktail shaker, shake all the ingredients, except the Champagne, with ice cubes, then fine-strain into a chilled coupe. Top up with the Champagne. Express the orange coin over the top, then discard.

✦ Charles H Baker Jr, *The Gentleman's Companion* (1939)

Stirred

&

Complex

Martini evolution

American wit Dorothy Parker put it best: 'I like to have a martini, two at the very most – after three I'm under the table, after four, I'm under my host.'

Every year, more than 13,000 Martinis are made at Claridge's, with seemingly limitless variations tailored to guests' preferences: a favourite gin or particular vodka; stirred or shaken; a little or large vermouth; olives, olive brine or a clean lemon twist.

A BRIEF HISTORY OF THE MARTINI

The origins of America's favourite cocktail are as murky as olive brine. In the mid-1800s, the first Martini-style cocktail that combined dark juniper-flavoured Dutch gin, bitters and sweet vermouth became popular. According to lore, it took inspiration from a story of a gold rush miner arriving in the town of Martinez, being told no Champagne was available and offered a special of the barkeep's own invention, which he promptly named after the town. Though another theory ties the drink to Martini & Rossi, Italian makers of vermouth who were exporting many bottles to the US at the time.

Towards the end of the 19th century, developments in distilling saw the rise first of an oft-sweetened 'Old Tom' gin, then of a variety closer to that drunk today: 'London dry' – a neutral grain spirit distilled with juniper as the predominant flavour. As drinkers embraced this innovation – and drier vermouths from France and Italy – the Martini's proportions began to change. Rather than a 1:1 split of gin and vermouth, the former began to dominate. As time went on, Martinis became drier – containing less vermouth – with famous preferred ratios including that of Ernest Hemingway, who drank his Martinis 15:1 gin to vermouth.

The vodka Martini appeared in the 1950s, drying the cocktail further (or, in many cases, removing the vermouth altogether), shortly before Ian Fleming had James Bond drink a Vesper (see page 68). The 1980s and 1990s saw the birth of the 'fruit Martini' (vodka, fruit liqueur and fruit juices), the Passionfruit Martini (see page 102) and the Pineapple Martini (see page 104). In later years, the vodka espresso, or Espresso Martini (see page 102), enjoyed a revival. In the past 20 years, tastes have changed again. A resurgence in classic cocktails, heightened interest in culinary trends and a rise in independent producers creating new spirits and vermouths have begun to steer preferences towards the classic Martini served at Claridge's today.

A MARTINI AT CLARIDGE'S

Claridge's guests often have preferred proportions for gin Martinis, such as 4:1 gin to vermouth, or 7:1. Vodka Martinis are typically 4:1, while Dirty Martinis (see page 44) replace the vermouth with olive brine. Many American guests skip the vermouth altogether.

When you drink a Martini at Claridge's, the gin, vodka and glass come straight from the freezer at -19°C (-2°F). At this temperature, the drink is exceptionally cold, creating a particular texture and viscosity. As it warms, it opens up, showcasing its aromas and botanicals.

A bespoke glass, similar to a coupette and designed by John Jenkins of Petersfield, Hampshire, is used at Claridge's. The crystal is so thin that, on first taste, the textures of glass and liquid almost unite. Using an atomizer, the bartender coats the glass evenly with three sprays of Noilly Prat vermouth, allowing the aromatics to bloom in the glass. They then slowly pour in 125ml (4fl oz) of the chosen gin or vodka, add the garnish – lemon twist, olives on a cocktail stick or, in the case of a Gibson (see page 70), cocktail onions – and serve immediately.

→ Claridge's Bar Martini (see page 44)

Martini

MAKES 1 DRINK

60ml (2fl oz) Claridge's London Dry
    Gin or Ketel One Vodka (or your
    preferred gin or vodka)
12.5ml (2½ tsp) Dolin Dry Vermouth
1 dash of orange bitters (if using gin
    and the lemon twist garnish)
Lemon twist or olive, to garnish

Stir all the ingredients in a mixing
glass, then strain into a chilled coupe.
Garnish with a lemon twist or an olive.

Dirty Martini

MAKES 1 DRINK

60ml (2fl oz) Ketel One Vodka (or
    your preferred vodka)
12.5ml (2½ tsp) olive brine
Olive, to garnish

Stir the vodka and olive brine in a
mixing glass, then strain into a chilled
coupe. Garnish with an olive.

Silver Bullet Martini

MAKES 1 DRINK

60ml (2fl oz) Plymouth Gin
10ml (¼fl oz) Wolfschmidt Kummel

Stir the gin and kümmel in a mixing
glass. Strain into a chilled coupe.

Claridge's Bar Martini

MAKES 1 DRINK

3 sprays of Noilly Prat Original Dry
    Vermouth
125ml (4fl oz) Claridge's London Dry
    Gin or Konik's Tail Vodka (or your
    preferred gin or vodka), frozen
Lemon twist or olive, to garnish

This is a much drier version of the
classic Martini (see above) and one
that guests at Claridge's enjoy the
most. The coupe and the gin or
vodka should be kept in the freezer
at −19°C (−2°F) and the garnish
prepared first to ensure the drink is
served as cold as possible.

When you're ready to serve, collect
the glass from the freezer and spray
with the vermouth. Pour in the gin or
vodka, garnish with a lemon twist or
an olive, and drink immediately.

The Painter's Room Sidecar

MAKES 1 DRINK

1 dash of Pernod Absinthe
2 drops of Saline Solution (see
    page 210)
2.5ml (½ tsp) Lustau Pedro Ximénez
    Sherry
35ml (1fl oz) Graham's Fine White
    Port
40ml (1½fl oz) Almond-infused Merlet
    Brothers Blend Cognac (see
    page 206)
Frozen grape, to garnish

Stir all the ingredients in a mixing
glass with ice cubes, then fine-strain
into a chilled Nick and Nora glass.
Garnish with a frozen grape on a
cocktail stick.

✦ Credit: Nathan McCarley-O'Neill,
The Painter's Room, London

Honey & Chamomile

MAKES 1 DRINK

5 drops of Saline Solution (see
    page 210)
4 dashes of Regans' Orange Bitters
5ml (1 tsp) Green Spot Single Pot Still
    Irish Whiskey
10ml (¼fl oz) Chamomile-infused
    Blossom Honey (see page 214)
50ml (2fl oz) Milk-infused Rye Batch
    (see page 205)

Stir all the ingredients in a mixing
glass with ice cubes for 8 to 10
rotations. Strain into a rocks glass
over an ice block.

✦ Credit: Nathan McCarley-O'Neill,
The Painter's Room, London

Oddjob

90ml (3fl oz) Saffron-infused Konik's
Tail Vodka (see page 207), frozen
10ml (¼fl oz) Sacred English Amber
Vermouth, frozen
5ml (1 tsp) Galliano l'Autentico, frozen
Orange twist, to garnish

As with the Claridge's Bar Martini
(see opposite), the liquid ingredients
and the coupe should be kept in
the freezer beforehand. Pour all the
frozen ingredients into the frozen
coupe, then garnish with an orange
twist.

✦ **Credit: Alessandro Palazzi, Dukes Bar,
London**

Bijou

MAKES 1 DRINK

35ml (1fl oz) Plymouth Gin
15ml (½fl oz) Green Chartreuse
20ml (¾fl oz) Martini Rosso
2 dashes of orange bitters
Lemon coin, to garnish
Fabbri Amarena cherry, to garnish

Stir all the ingredients in a mixing
glass, then strain into a chilled coupe.
Express the lemon coin over the top,
then discard. Garnish with the cherry.

✦ **Credit: *Harry Johnson's Bartender's
Manual* (1882)**

Greenpoint

MAKES 1 DRINK

50ml (2fl oz) Michter's US*1 Kentucky
Straight Rye Whiskey
12.5ml (2½ tsp) Yellow Chartreuse
12.5ml (2½ tsp) Martini Rosso
2 dashes of Angostura bitters
1 dash of orange bitters
Lemon twist, to garnish

Stir all the ingredients in a mixing
glass, then strain into a chilled coupe.
Garnish with a lemon twist.

✦ **Credit: Michael McIlroy, Milk & Honey,
New York**

Bentley

MAKES 1 DRINK

50ml (2fl oz) Adrien Camut 6 Year Old
Calvados
25ml (1fl oz) Martini Rosso
1 dash of Pernod Absinthe
1 dash of orange bitters
Lemon twist, to garnish

Stir all the ingredients in a mixing
glass, then strain into a chilled coupe.
Garnish with a lemon twist.

✦ **Credit: Harry Craddock, The Savoy,
London**

Martinez

MAKES 1 DRINK

40ml (1½fl oz) Boatyard Old Tom Gin
30ml (1fl oz) Martini Rosso
7.5ml (1½ tsp) Cointreau
7.5ml (1½ tsp) Maraschino
2 dashes of orange bitters
1 dash of Angostura bitters
Lemon coin, to garnish
Fabbri Amarena cherry, to garnish

Stir all the ingredients in a mixing
glass with ice cubes, then strain into
a chilled coupe. Express the lemon
coin over the top, then discard.
Garnish with the cherry.

Delmonico

MAKES 1 DRINK

50ml (2fl oz) Rémy Martin VSOP
Cognac
20ml (¾fl oz) Martini Rosso
2 dashes of Angostura bitters
Fabbri Amarena cherry, to garnish

Stir all the ingredients in a mixing
glass with ice cubes, then strain into
a chilled coupe. Garnish with the
cherry.

✦ **Credit: Delmonico's Restaurant, New York**

Trinity

MAKES 1 DRINK

25ml (1fl oz) Plymouth Gin
25ml (1fl oz) Carpano Antica Formula
    Vermouth
20ml (¾fl oz) Dolin Dry Vermouth
Lemon twist, to garnish

Stir all the ingredients in a mixing glass, then strain into a chilled coupe. Garnish with a lemon twist.

Brooks Street

MAKES 1 DRINK

2 orange coins
40ml (1½fl oz) Jensen's Old Tom Gin
25ml (1fl oz) Carpano Antica Formula
    Vermouth
2 dashes of Angostura bitters
Lemon twist, to garnish

Express the orange coins over the top of a mixing glass, then discard. Add the remaining ingredients and a handful of ice cubes and stir. Strain into a chilled coupe and garnish with a lemon twist.

✦ Credit: Davide Cade, Claridge's Bar, London

William Wallace

MAKES 1 DRINK

50ml (2fl oz) Chivas Regal 12 Year Old
    Blended Scotch Whisky
10ml (¼fl oz) Asterley Bros Estate
    Sweet Vermouth
10ml (¼fl oz) Lustau Pedro Ximénez
    Sherry
3 dashes of orange bitters
Orange coin, to garnish

Stir all the ingredients in a mixing glass, then strain into a chilled coupe. Garnish with an orange coin.

✦ Credit: Joe Schofield, Schofield's Bar, Manchester

Padrino

MAKES 1 DRINK

40ml (1½fl oz) Michter's US*1
    Kentucky Straight Rye Whiskey
15ml (½fl oz) Disaronno Amaretto
10ml (¼fl oz) Lustau Oloroso Sherry
10ml (¼fl oz) Lustau Fino Sherry
5ml (1 tsp) Merlet Lune d'Abricot
2 dashes of Peychaud's bitters
Lemon twist, to garnish

Stir all the ingredients in a mixing glass, then strain into a chilled rocks glass over an ice block. Garnish with a lemon twist.

✦ Credit: Daniel Schofield, Schofield's Bar, Manchester

→ Brooks Street

Rob Roy

MAKES 1 DRINK

50ml (2fl oz) Johnnie Walker Black
    Label Whisky
25ml (1fl oz) Martini Rosso
2 dashes of Angostura bitters
Fabbri Amarena cherry, to garnish

Stir all the ingredients in a mixing
glass with ice cubes, then strain into
a chilled rocks glass. Garnish with the
cherry.

✦ Credit: Waldorf-Astoria, New York

Godfather

MAKES 1 DRINK

60ml (2fl oz) The Lakes The One Fine
    Blended Whisky
20ml (¾fl oz) Disaronno Amaretto
Orange twist, to garnish

Stir the whisky and Amaretto in
a mixing glass, then strain into a
chilled rocks glass over an ice block.
Garnish with an orange twist.

American Trilogy

MAKES 1 DRINK

25ml (1fl oz) Adrien Camut 6 Year Old
    Calvados
25ml (1fl oz) Michter's US*1 Kentucky
    Straight Rye Whiskey
2 dashes of orange bitters
10ml (¼fl oz) sugar syrup (see page 21)
Orange twist, to garnish

Stir all the ingredients in a mixing
glass, then strain into a chilled rocks
glass over an ice block. Garnish with
an orange twist.

✦ Credit: Michael McIlroy & Richard
Boccato, Little Branch, New York

Clave

MAKES 1 DRINK

2 dashes of Tarragon Bitters (see
    page 206)
2.5ml (½ tsp) Ælred Melonade
2.5ml (½ tsp) Briottet Tres Vieux Marc
    de Bourgogne
10ml (¼fl oz) Gonzalez Byass Del
    Duque Amontillado 30 Year Old
    Sherry
10ml (¼fl oz) Château De Beaulon
    Pineau Des Charentes Blanc 10
    Year Old
40ml (1½fl oz) Belvedere Vodka

Stir all the ingredients in a mixing
glass with ice cubes for 8 to 10
rotations. Strain into a rocks glass
over an ice block.

✦ Credit: Nathan McCarley-O'Neill,
The Painter's Room, London

El Presidente

MAKES 1 DRINK

30ml (1fl oz) Havana Club Especial
    Rum
20ml (¾fl oz) Dolin Vermouth Blanc
7.5ml (1½ tsp) Combier Triple Sec
5ml (1 tsp) Bristol Syrup Company
    Grenadine
2.5ml (½ tsp) sugar syrup (see
    page 21)
Orange twist, to garnish

Stir all the ingredients in a mixing
glass, then strain into a chilled coupe.
Garnish with an orange twist.

✦ Credit: John B Escalante, *Manual del
Cantinero* (1915)

Toronto

MAKES 1 DRINK

50ml (2fl oz) Knob Creek Rye Whiskey
10ml (¼fl oz) Fernet-Branca
10ml (¼fl oz) sugar syrup (see page 21)
2 dashes of Angostura bitters
Orange twist, to garnish

Stir all the ingredients in a mixing
glass, then strain into a chilled rocks
glass over an ice block. Garnish with
an orange twist.

Harvard

MAKES 1 DRINK

50ml (2fl oz) Merlet Brothers Blend
    Cognac
25ml (1fl oz) Martini Rosso
2 dashes of orange bitters
1 dash of sugar syrup (see page 21)
Orange coin, to garnish

Stir all the ingredients in a mixing
glass, then strain into a chilled coupe.
Garnish with an orange coin.

✦ Credit: George J Kappeler, *Modern
American Drinks* (1906)

The Painter's Room Martini

MAKES 1 DRINK

3 dashes of Japanese Ceremonial
    Matcha Bitters (see page 214)
2.5ml (½ tsp) Dolin Vermouth Blanc
2.5ml (½ tsp) Noilly Prat Original Dry
    Vermouth
30ml (1fl oz) Tanqueray London
    Dry Gin
30ml (1fl oz) Plymouth Gin
Lemon twist, to garnish
Olive, to garnish

Stir all the ingredients in a mixing
glass with ice cubes, then strain into
a chilled coupe. Garnish with a lemon
twist and olive.

✦ Credit: Nathan McCarley-O'Neill,
The Painter's Room, London

Remember the Maine

MAKES 1 DRINK

45ml (1½fl oz) Knob Creek Rye
    Whiskey
15ml (½fl oz) Carpano Antica Formula
    Vermouth
10ml (¼fl oz) Heering Cherry Liqueur
2 dashes of Angostura bitters
1 dash of Pernod Absinthe
Orange coin, to garnish

Stir all the ingredients in a mixing
glass, then strain into a chilled coupe.
Express the orange coin over the top,
then discard.

✦ Adapted from: Charles H Baker Jr,
The Gentleman's Companion (1939)

Ode to the negroni

A well-made negroni represents true harmony: three notes – gin, Campari, vermouth – in perfect proportion. Author Kingsley Amis singled it out for one simple reason: 'It has the power, rare with drinks and indeed everything else, of cheering you up.'

With its conspicuous red clarity and bitter taste, the negroni is one of the world's most popular cocktails. A Claridge's negroni is served in a golden ratio. First, 25ml (1fl oz) gin – the base spirit, for body, juniper and citrus. Then 25ml (1fl oz) vermouth – more body, plus a little sweetness and bitterness. Finally, 25ml (1fl oz) Campari – bitterness, a little sweetness and entirely right to finish the drink.

A Claridge's negroni is built straight into the serving glass over an ice block, rather than using a mixing glass, as the latter method risks over-diluting the drink. It also allows the flavours to develop in the glass: a negroni, after all, is a contemplative drink, made for slow sipping. As you drink, you will find your negroni matures and gains in complexity, though sadly your conversation may not follow a similar pattern. As Anthony Bourdain noted after a negroni-fuelled party, 'those things hit you like a freight train after four or five.'

The negroni's simplicity makes it versatile. Different gins and vermouths alter the taste. Gin may be exchanged for whisky, to make a Boulevardier (see page 74), or tequila. Or you might infuse your Campari to change its dynamics. Throughout this book are twists on the formula, from The Painter's Room Negroni (see page 56) to the White Negroni (see page 54) and the Coffee Boulevardier (see page 74).

In 2019, Claridge's celebrated the centennial of the negroni (reportedly created in 1919 at Florence's Caffè Casoni by Fosco Scarselli). At Claridge's Bar, five versions were served: the Third Time Lucky (see page 38), a spin on a Negroni Sbagliato (see page 26), the Crown Jewel (made with all-British ingredients and Beefeater Crown Jewel gin), a whisky negroni with peanut-infused Campari, and the Fragola, with gin, rum and strawberry sherbet, served straight up (see page 74). At nineteen minutes past seven each evening, the whole bar was offered a miniature Fumoir Negroni (see page 54). Scarselli, one imagines, would have approved.

Traditional negronis will always be available at Claridge's. However, next time you visit, try a Fumoir Negroni, with chamomile-infused gin and coffee-infused vermouth. Coffee adds a deliciously rich depth, while chamomile-infused gin is a nod to the Fumoir's proximity to the Foyer. Those having afternoon tea next door will often order a cocktail to finish, and a Fumoir Negroni can complement a 4pm cucumber sandwich as finely as it does a late-night *tête-à-tête* in a far corner of the bar.

→ **Overleaf, left to right**
White Negroni (see page 54)
Old Pal (see page 60)
The Painter's Room Negroni (see page 56)
Fumoir Negroni (see page 54)
Boulevardier (see page 74)

Negroni

MAKES 1 DRINK

25ml (1fl oz) Plymouth Gin
25ml (1fl oz) Carpano Antica Formula Vermouth
25ml (1fl oz) Campari
Orange slice, to garnish

Build the ingredients in a chilled rocks glass over an ice block, then stir to dilute. Garnish with a slice of orange.

Rhubarb Negroni

(Davies and Brook)

MAKES 1 DRINK

---

2 dashes of Saline Solution (see page 210)
3 dashes of Muyu Jasmine Verte
20ml (¾fl oz) Carpano Antica Formula Vermouth
20ml (¾fl oz) Amaro Ramazzotti
30ml (1fl oz) D&B Rhubarb Cordial (see page 193)
25ml (1fl oz) Casamigos Blanco Tequila
Rhubarb coin, to garnish

Build the ingredients in a chilled rocks glass over an ice block, then stir for 8 to 10 rotations. Garnish with a rhubarb coin.

✦ **Credit: Matteo Carretta**

White Negroni

MAKES 1 DRINK

25ml (1fl oz) Plymouth Gin
25ml (1fl oz) Lillet Blanc
25ml (1fl oz) Suze
Grapefruit twist, to garnish

Stir all the ingredients in a mixing glass, then strain into a chilled rocks glass over an ice block. Garnish with a grapefruit twist.

Coconut Negroni

MAKES 1 DRINK

20ml (¾fl oz) Fig Leaf-infused Mancino Vermouth Rosso Amaranto (see page 203)
30ml (1fl oz) Coconut-infused Campari (see page 202)
25ml (1fl oz) Tanqueray London Dry Gin
2 dashes of Saline Solution (see page 210)
Orange twist, to garnish

Stir all the ingredients in a mixing glass, then strain into a chilled rocks glass over an ice block. Garnish with an orange twist.

✦ **Credit: Darren Leaney, Capitano, Melbourne**

Mezcal Negroni

MAKES 1 DRINK

25ml (1fl oz) Koch Espadín Mezcal
25ml (1fl oz) Campari
25ml (1fl oz) Carpano Antica Formula Vermouth
Orange slice, to serve

Stir all the ingredients in a mixing glass, then strain into a chilled rocks glass over an ice block. Garnish with a slice of orange.

Fumoir Negroni

MAKES 1 DRINK

25ml (1fl oz) Chamomile-infused Hepple Gin (see page 202)
25ml (1fl oz) Campari
25ml (1fl oz) Coffee-infused Carpano Antica Formula Vermouth (see page 203)
7.5ml (1½ tsp) Punt e Mes Vermouth
Orange twist, to garnish

Stir all the ingredients in a mixing glass, then strain into a chilled rocks glass over an ice block. Garnish with an orange twist.

✦ **Credit: Oliver Blackburn, The Fumoir, London**

→ **Rhubarb Negroni**

Mandarin Negroni

MAKES 1 DRINK

30ml (1fl oz) Beefeater London Dry Gin
25ml (1fl oz) Carpano Antica Formula Vermouth
25ml (1fl oz) Mandarin & Cranberry-infused Campari (see page 204)
Mandarin segment, to garnish

Stir all the ingredients in a mixing glass, then strain into a chilled rocks glass over an ice block. Garnish with a mandarin segment.

✦ **Credit: Nathan McCarley-O'Neill, Davies and Brook, London**

Psycho Killer

MAKES 1 DRINK

60ml (2fl oz) Redbreast 12 Year Old Whiskey
20ml (¾fl oz) Campari
15ml (½fl oz) Giffard Crème de Cacao (white)
15ml (½fl oz) Giffard Banane du Brésil
2 dashes of Pernod Absinthe
Orange coin, to garnish

Stir all the ingredients in a mixing glass, then strain into a chilled coupe. Express the orange coin over the top, then discard.

✦ **Credit: Jillian Vose, The Dead Rabbit, New York**

The Painter's Room Negroni

MAKES 1 DRINK

2 dashes of Angostura bitters
15ml (½fl oz) Punt e Mes Vermouth
15ml (½fl oz) Mancino Vermouth Rosso Amaranto
15ml (½fl oz) The Lakes Gin
30ml (1fl oz) Campari
Orange slice, to garnish

Build the ingredients in a large rocks glass over an ice block. Stir for 15 rotations until the glass and the liquid are chilled. Garnish with an orange slice.

Sazerac

MAKES 1 DRINK

30ml (1fl oz) Rémy Martin VSOP Cognac
30ml (1fl oz) Michter's US*1 Kentucky Straight Rye Whiskey
10ml (¼fl oz) sugar syrup (see page 21)
2 dashes of Peychaud's bitters
1 dash of Angostura bitters
6 sprays of Pernod Absinthe
Orange coin, to garnish
Lemon coin, to garnish

Stir all the ingredients, except the absinthe, in a mixing glass. Spritz the inside of the glass with 6 light sprays of absinthe, using an atomizer, then strain into a chilled large rocks glass. Express the orange and lemon coins over the top, then discard.

Right Hand

MAKES 1 DRINK

40ml (1½fl oz) El Dorado 15 Year Old Rum
20ml (¾fl oz) Carpano Antica Formula Vermouth
20ml (¾fl oz) Campari
5 dashes of Bob's Chocolate Bitters
Orange twist, to garnish

Stir all the ingredients in a mixing glass, then strain into a chilled rocks glass over an ice block. Garnish with an orange twist.

✦ **Credit: Michael McIlroy, Milk & Honey, New York**

➜ **Mandarin Negroni**

Black Manhattan

MAKES 1 DRINK

50ml (2fl oz) Maker's Mark Bourbon
    Whisky
25ml (1fl oz) Amaro Averna
1 dash of Angostura bitters
Orange twist, to garnish

Stir all the ingredients in a mixing
glass, then strain into a chilled coupe.
Garnish with an orange twist.

Money Honey

MAKES 1 DRINK

40ml (1½fl oz) Banana-infused
    Macallan Whisky (see page 201)
25ml (1fl oz) Banana Wine (see
    page 209)
20ml (¾fl oz) Tonka Bean-infused
    Noilly Prat Ambré Vermouth (see
    page 207)

Stir all the ingredients in a mixing
glass. Strain into a chilled rocks glass
over an ice block.

✦ **Credit: Yann Bouvignies, Scarfes Bar,
London**

Manhattan

MAKES 1 DRINK

50ml (2fl oz) Maker's Mark Bourbon
    Whisky
25ml (1fl oz) Carpano Antica Formula
    Vermouth
1 dash of Angostura bitters
Orange coin, to garnish
Fabbri Amarena cherry, to garnish

Stir all the ingredients in a mixing
glass with ice cubes, then strain
into a chilled coupe. Express the
orange coin over the top, then
discard. Garnish with the cherry
on a cocktail stick.

Rum & Cherry

MAKES 1 DRINK

40ml (1½fl oz) Cherry-infused
    Diplomático Planas Rum (see
    page 202)
10ml (¼fl oz) Sonoma County 2nd
    Chance Wheat Whiskey
10ml (¼fl oz) Bay Leaf-infused
    Belvedere Vodka (see page 201)
10ml (¼fl oz) Lapsang Souchong
    Syrup (see page 195)

Stir all the ingredients in a mixing
glass. Strain into a chilled coupe.

✦ **Credit: Alessandro Villa, Fera at
Claridge's, London**

Hanky Panky

MAKES 1 DRINK

35ml (1fl oz) Plymouth Gin
30ml (1fl oz) Martini Rosso
5ml (1 tsp) Fernet-Branca
Orange coin, to garnish

Stir all the ingredients in a mixing
glass, then strain into a chilled coupe.
Garnish with an orange coin.

✦ **Credit: Ada Coleman, The Savoy, London**

→ Manhattan

Old Pal

MAKES 1 DRINK

25ml (1fl oz) Michter's US*1 Kentucky
Straight Rye Whiskey
25ml (1fl oz) Dolin Dry Vermouth
25ml (1fl oz) Campari
Orange coin, to garnish

Stir all the ingredients in a mixing
glass, then strain into a chilled coupe.
Garnish with an orange coin.

✦ Credit: Harry MacElhone, Harry's Bar,
Paris

Bobby Burns

MAKES 1 DRINK

50ml (2fl oz) Chivas Regal 12 Year Old
Blended Scotch Whisky
20ml (¾fl oz) Carpano Antica Formula
Vermouth
7.5ml (1½ tsp) Bénédictine
Lemon twist, to garnish

Stir all the ingredients in a mixing
glass, then strain into a chilled coupe.
Garnish with a lemon twist.

✦ Credit: Harry Craddock, The Savoy,
London

Duke of Gordon

MAKES 1 DRINK

25ml (1fl oz) Glenlivet 18 Year Old
Single Malt Scotch Whisky
25ml (1fl oz) Powers John's Lane 12
Year Old Irish Whiskey
5ml (1 tsp) Laphroaig 10 Year Old
Whisky
5ml (1 tsp) Maraschino
3 dashes of Pernod Absinthe
2 dashes of orange bitters
Orange coin, to garnish

Stir all the ingredients in a mixing
glass with ice cubes, then strain
into a chilled rocks glass over an ice
block. Garnish with an orange coin.

✦ Credit: Nathan McCarley-O'Neill,
Claridge's Bar, London

Earth Laddie

MAKES 1 DRINK

35ml (1fl oz) Bruichladdich The Classic
Laddie Whisky
15ml (½fl oz) Tío Pepe Dos Palmas
Fino Sherry
25ml (1fl oz) Fermented Apple (see
page 214)
25ml (1fl oz) Parsnip & Thyme Cordial
(see page 193)

Build the ingredients in a chilled
highball over an ice block and stir
gently.

✦ Credit: Martin Siska, Scarfes Bar, London

Piña Clara

MAKES 1 DRINK

Lime coin, plus an extra coin, to
garnish
35ml (1fl oz) Coconut Butter-washed
Bacardí Heritage (see page 202)
35ml (1fl oz) Clarified Pineapple Juice
(see page 210)
5ml (1 tsp) coconut syrup

Express the lime coin over the top
of a mixing glass, then discard. Add
the remaining ingredients, and stir
with ice cubes. Strain into a chilled
vintage coupe. Garnish with another
lime coin.

✦ Credit: Gábor Onufer, The Fumoir,
London

The Painter's Room Old Fashioned

MAKES 1 DRINK

2 dashes of Angostura bitters
4 drops of Saline Solution (see page 210)
10ml (¼fl oz) maple syrup
5ml (1 tsp) Capreolus Quince Eau de Vie
20ml (¾fl oz) The Lakes The One Fine Blended Whisky
30ml (1fl oz) Cultured Butter-infused Whisky (see page 206)

Stir all the ingredients in a mixing glass with ice cubes for 8 to 10 rotations. Strain into a rocks glass over an ice block.

✦ Credit: Nathan McCarley-O'Neill, The Painter's Room, London

Popcorn Old Fashioned

MAKES 1 DRINK

50ml (2fl oz) Popcorn-infused Suntory Chita Whisky (see page 207)
5ml (1 tsp) sugar syrup (see page 21)
2 dashes of Angostura bitters
Orange twist, to garnish

Stir all the ingredients in a mixing glass with ice cubes, then strain into a chilled rocks glass over an ice block. Garnish with an orange twist.

✦ Credit: James Hawkins, Sexy Fish, London

Rum Old Fashioned

MAKES 1 DRINK

50ml (2fl oz) El Dorado 15 Year Old Rum
10ml (¼fl oz) sugar syrup (see page 21)
3 dashes of Angostura bitters
Orange twist, to garnish

Stir all the ingredients in a mixing glass, then strain into a chilled rocks glass over an ice block. Garnish with an orange twist.

Old Fashioned

MAKES 1 DRINK

50ml (2fl oz) Maker's Mark Bourbon Whisky
10ml (¼fl oz) sugar syrup (see page 21)
2 dashes of Angostura bitters
Orange twist, to garnish

Stir all the ingredients in a mixing glass with ice cubes, then strain into a chilled rocks glass over an ice block. Garnish with an orange twist.

Oaxacan Old Fashioned

MAKES 1 DRINK

45ml (1½fl oz) Tapatio Blanco Tequila
15ml (½fl oz) Del Maguey Chichicapa
    Mezcal
10ml (¼fl oz) agave syrup
2 dashes of Angostura bitters
Orange twist, to garnish

Stir all the ingredients in a mixing
glass, then strain into a chilled rocks
glass over an ice block. Garnish with
an orange twist.

✦ Credit: Phil Ward, Death & Co,
New York

Maple Old Fashioned

MAKES 1 DRINK

30ml (1fl oz) Michter's US*1 Kentucky
    Straight Rye Whiskey
20ml (¾fl oz) Lustau Amontillado
    Sherry
15ml (½fl oz) Suntory Toki Whisky
7ml (1½ tsp) Bénédictine
15ml (½fl oz) St Lawrence Gold Pure
    Maple Syrup
5ml (1 tsp) verjus
3 dashes of Angostura bitters
4 dashes of Saline Solution (see
    page 210)

Stir all the ingredients in a mixing
glass. Strain into a chilled rocks glass
over an ice block.

✦ Credit: Pietro Collina, Davies and Brook,
London

Green Fig Old Fashioned

MAKES 1 DRINK

60ml (2fl oz) Green Fig-infused
    Michter's Bourbon (see
    page 204)
15ml (½fl oz) Lustau Oloroso Sherry
15ml (½fl oz) Rooibos Syrup (see
    page 196)
7.5ml (1½ tsp) Lustau Pedro Ximénez
    Sherry
3 dashes of Bob's Chocolate Bitters
Green fig slice, to garnish

Stir all the ingredients in a mixing
glass. Strain into a chilled rocks glass
over an ice block. Garnish with a slice
of geen fig.

✦ Credit: Nathan McCarley-O'Neill, Davies
and Brook, London

Broadway

MAKES 1 DRINK

40ml (1½fl oz) Michter's US*1
    Kentucky Straight Rye Whiskey
10ml (¼fl oz) Bonal Gentiane-Quina
5ml (1 tsp) Maraschino
2.5ml (½ tsp) St Lawrence Gold Pure
    Maple Syrup
1 dash of Angostura bitters
1 dash of orange bitters
Fabbri Amarena cherry, to garnish

Stir the ingredients in a mixing glass
with ice cubes. Strain into a chilled
rocks glass over an ice block and
garnish with the cherry.

✦ Credit: Nathan McCarley-O'Neill,
Claridge's Bar, London

→ Overleaf, left to right
   American Trilogy (see page 48)
   Broadway (see page 62)
   Green Fig Old Fashioned
      (see above)
   Duke of Gordon (see page 60)

Raspberries & Tea

MAKES 1 DRINK

5 raspberries, plus 4 extra raspberries,
   cut in half, to garnish
40ml (1½fl oz) Berkshire Botanical
   Dry Gin
20ml (¾fl oz) Svöl Danish-Style
   Aquavit
25ml (1fl oz) Cinzano Bianco
   Vermouth
5ml (1 tsp) Capreolus Raspberry Eau
   de Vie
35ml (1fl oz) lemon verbena tea
7.5ml (1½ tsp) orange blossom honey
5ml (1 tsp) Womersley Raspberry
   Vinegar
4 dashes of Saline Solution (see
   page 210)
3 dashes of orange bitters
2 dashes of Malic Acid Solution (see
   page 209)
Lemon verbena leaves, to garnish

Gently break the raspberries
apart, without bursting the seeds,
and combine with the remaining
ingredients in a sous-vide vacuum
bag or airtight container. Place in the
refrigerator for 2 hours.

Fine-strain into a mixing glass. Stir
with ice cubes, then serve in a teacup
with lemon verbena leaves at the
bottom and garnished with 4 halved
raspberries.

✦ Inspired by: A Taste of Noma
pop-up at Claridge's
Credit: Denis Broci, Claridge's Bar,
London

Pink Gin

MAKES 1 DRINK

50ml (2fl oz) Plymouth Gin, frozen
3 dashes of Angostura bitters
Lemon coin, to garnish

Build the gin and Angostura bitters
in a chilled rocks glass over an ice
block, then stir for 40 seconds.
Express the lemon coin over the top,
then discard.

Coconut
(Davies and Brook)

MAKES 1 DRINK

Freeze dried raspberry powder
65ml (2¼fl oz) Coconut Batch (see
   page 201)

Rim the outside of a chilled coupe
with freeze dried raspberry powder
(see page 19), so that the glass
and stem are fully coated. Stir the
coconut batch in a mixing glass with
ice cubes, then strain into the coupe.

✦ Credit: Nathan McCarley-O'Neill

Tipperary

MAKES 1 DRINK

35ml (1fl oz) Redbreast 12 Year Old
    Whiskey
10ml (¼fl oz) Green Chartreuse
20ml (¾fl oz) Carpano Antica Formula
    Vermouth
2 dashes of orange bitters
Lemon coin, to garnish

Stir all the ingredients in a mixing
glass, then strain into a chilled coupe.
Garnish with a lemon coin.

✦ Credit: Hugo R Ensslin, *Recipes for Mixed
Drinks* (1916 & 1917)

Corpse Reviver No 1

MAKES 1 DRINK

25ml (1fl oz) Adrien Camut 6 Year Old
    Calvados
25ml (1fl oz) Rémy Martin VSOP
    Cognac
25ml (1fl oz) Martini Rosso
1 dash of Angostura bitters

Stir all the ingredients in a mixing
glass. Strain into a chilled coupe.

✦ Credit: Harry Craddock, The Savoy,
London

The Royal Stag

MAKES 1 DRINK

40ml (1½fl oz) The Dalmore 15
20ml (¾fl oz) Sweet Vermouth Blend
    (see page 210)
20ml (¾fl oz) Campari
2 dashes of Bénédictine
2 dashes of Bob's Chocolate Bitters
1 dash of Roasted Almond Tincture
    (see page 199)
Square of 75% dark chocolate, to
    garnish

Stir all the ingredients in a mixing
glass, then strain into a chilled rocks
glass over an ice block. Garnish with
a square of chocolate.

✦ Credit: Denis Broci, Claridge's Bar,
London

Vesper

MAKES 1 DRINK

50ml (2fl oz) Plymouth Gin
20ml (¾fl oz) Ketel One Vodka
10ml (¼fl oz) Lillet Blanc
Lemon twist, to garnish

In a cocktail shaker, shake all the
ingredients with ice cubes, then
strain into a chilled coupe. Garnish
with a lemon twist.

✦ Credit: Ian Fleming

Vieux Carre

MAKES 1 DRINK

25ml (1fl oz) Rémy Martin VSOP
    Cognac
20ml (¾fl oz) Michter's US*1
    Kentucky Straight Rye Whiskey
20ml (¾fl oz) Carpano Antica Formula
    Vermouth
7.5ml (1½ tsp) Bénédictine
1 dash of Peychaud's bitters
1 dash of Angostura bitters
Lemon twist, to garnish

Stir all the ingredients in a mixing
glass, then strain into a chilled rocks
glass over an ice block. Garnish with
a lemon twist.

✦ Credit: Walter Bergeron, Carousel Bar,
New Orleans

→ **The Royal Stag**

Angel Face

MAKES 1 DRINK

30ml (1fl oz) Plymouth Gin
20ml (¾fl oz) Adrien Camut 6 Year
    Old Calvados
20ml (¾fl oz) Briottet Crème
    d'Abricot
Lemon twist, to garnish

Stir all the ingredients in a mixing
glass, then strain into a chilled coupe.
Garnish with a lemon twist.

✦ Credit: Harry Craddock, The Savoy,
London

Dynasty

MAKES 1 DRINK

40ml (1½fl oz) Belvedere Vodka
5ml (1 tsp) Merlet Crème de Cassis
5ml (1 tsp) Saffron-infused Cocchi
    Americano (see page 205)
1 dash of Bob's Lavender Bitters

Stir all the ingredients in a mixing
glass. Strain into a chilled coupe.

✦ Credit: Nathan McCarley-O'Neill,
The Painter's Room, London

Three Kingdoms

MAKES 1 DRINK

25ml (1fl oz) Michter's US*1 Kentucky
    Straight Rye Whiskey
20ml (¾fl oz) Bacardí 8 Year Old Rum
45ml (1½fl oz) Cocchi Rosa
5ml (1 tsp) Apricot Reduction (see
    page 209)
1 dash of Pernod Absinthe
Orange coin, to garnish

Stir all the ingredients in a mixing
glass, then strain into a chilled Nick
and Nora glass. Express the orange
coin over the top, then discard.

✦ Credit: Denis Broci, Claridge's Bar,
London

Montgomery

MAKES 1 DRINK

75ml (2½fl oz) Plymouth Gin
5ml (1 tsp) Noilly Pratt Original Dry
    Vermouth
Lemon twist, to garnish

Stir all the ingredients in a mixing
glass, then strain into a chilled coupe.
Garnish with a lemon twist.

✦ Enjoyed by: Ernest Hemingway
Named after: Field Marshal Bernard Law
Montgomery

Gibson

MAKES 1 DRINK

60ml (2fl oz) Plymouth Gin
10ml (¼fl oz) Dolin Dry Vermouth
3 cocktail onions, to garnish

Stir the gin and vermouth in a mixing
glass, then strain into a chilled coupe.
Garnish with the cocktail onions.

Behind the Painted Screen

MAKES 1 DRINK

30ml (1fl oz) Boatyard Double Gin
30ml (1fl oz) Dubonnet
20ml (¾fl oz) Campari
5ml (1 tsp) kümmel

Stir all the ingredients in a mixing glass. Strain into a chilled rocks glass over an ice block.

✦ **Credit: Declan McGurk, The Boatyard Distillery, Enniskillen, Northern Ireland**

Valley of the Deer

MAKES 1 DRINK

35ml (1fl oz) Glenfiddich Grand Cru 23 Year Old Whisky
15ml (½fl oz) Capreolus Perry Pear Eau de Vie
7.5ml (1½ tsp) St Lawrence Gold Pure Maple Syrup
5ml (1 tsp) Disaronno Amaretto
3 dashes of Bob's Chocolate Bitters
Orange twist, to garnish

Stir all the ingredients in a mixing glass, then strain into a chilled rocks glass over an ice block. Garnish with an orange twist.

✦ **Credit: Nathan McCarley-O'Neill, Claridge's Bar, London**

Journalist

MAKES 1 DRINK

50ml (2fl oz) Plymouth Gin
12.5ml (2½ tsp) Martini Rosso
12.5ml (2½ tsp) Martini Bianco
2.5ml (½ tsp) Pierre Ferrand Dry Curaçao
2.5ml (½ tsp) lemon juice
2 dashes of Angostura bitters
2 dashes of orange bitters
Lemon twist, to garnish

Stir all the ingredients in a mixing glass, then strain into a chilled coupe. Garnish with a lemon twist.

✦ **Credit: Harry Craddock, The Savoy, London**

Left Hand

MAKES 1 DRINK

40ml (1½fl oz) Maker's Mark Bourbon Whisky
20ml (¾fl oz) Carpano Antica Formula Vermouth
20ml (¾fl oz) Campari
5 dashes of Bob's Chocolate Bitters
Orange twist, to garnish

Stir all the ingredients in a mixing glass, then strain into a chilled rocks glass over an ice block. Garnish with an orange twist.

✦ **Credit: Sam Ross, Attaboy, New York**

Gimlet

MAKES 1 DRINK

50ml (2fl oz) Plymouth Gin
25ml (1fl oz) Rose's Lime Juice Cordial

Stir the gin and cordial in a mixing glass. Strain into a chilled coupe.

Creole Cocktail

50ml (2fl oz) Michter's US*1 Kentucky
    Straight Rye Whiskey
12.5ml (2½ tsp) Carpano Antica
    Formula Vermouth
7.5ml (1½ tsp) Bénédictine
7.5ml (1½ tsp) Amer Picon
2 dashes of Peychaud's bitters
Lemon twist, to garnish

Stir all the ingredients in a mixing
glass, then strain into a chilled coupe.
Garnish with a lemon twist.

Weasel

MAKES 1 DRINK

40ml (1½fl oz) Hepple Gin
10ml (¼fl oz) Dolin Dry Vermouth
10ml (¼fl oz) Bay Leaf Syrup (see
    page 195)
1 drop of Citric Acid Solution (see
    page 210)
Grapefruit coin, to garnish

Stir all the ingredients in a mixing
glass with ice cubes, then strain
into a chilled coupe. Garnish with a
grapefruit coin.

✦ Credit: Nathan McCarley-O'Neill,
Claridge's Bar, London

Bohemian Rhapsody

MAKES 1 DRINK

25ml (1fl oz) Redbreast 15 Year Old
    Whiskey
25ml (1fl oz) Martell Cordon Bleu
    Cognac
25ml (1fl oz) Lustau Pedro Ximénez
    Sherry
1 dash of Citric Acid Solution (see
    page 210)
1 dash of Angostura bitters
Fabbri Amarena cherry, to garnish

Stir all the ingredients in a mixing
glass, then strain into a chilled Nick
and Nora glass. Garnish with the
cherry.

✦ Credit: Paolo Perrini, The Fumoir, London

Widow's Kiss

MAKES 1 DRINK

50ml (2fl oz) Adrien Camut 6 Year Old
    Calvados
10ml (¼fl oz) Yellow Chartreuse
10ml (¼fl oz) Bénédictine
2 dashes of Angostura bitters
Fabbri Amarena cherry, to garnish

Stir all the ingredients in a mixing
glass with ice cubes, then strain into
a chilled coupe. Garnish with the
cherry on a cocktail stick.

✦ Credit: George J Kappeler, Holland
House, New York

D&B Manhattan
(Davies and Brook)

MAKES 1 DRINK

1 dash Angostura bitters
1 dash Angostura Orange Bitters
2.5ml (½ tsp) Bristol Syrup Company
    Simple 1:1
5ml (1 tsp) Merlet Lune d'Abricot
20ml (¾fl oz) Cocchi Storico
    Vermouth Di Torino
25ml (1fl oz) Hennessy VSOP Privilège
    Cognac
25ml (1fl oz) Michter's US*1 Kentucky
    Straight Bourbon Whiskey
Almonds, sliced, to garnish
Dried apricots, to garnish
Fabbri Amarena cherry, to garnish

Stir all the ingredients in a mixing
glass with ice cubes, then fine-strain
into a chilled Nick & Nora glass.
Garnish with sliced almonds, dried
apricots and the cherry.

✦ Credit: Matteo Carretta

→ D&B Manhattan

Fragola

MAKES 1 DRINK

30ml (1fl oz) Plymouth Gin
20ml (¾fl oz) Havana Club Selección
    de Maestros Rum
20ml (¾fl oz) Cocchi Rosa
5ml (1 tsp) Strawberry Sherbet (see
    page 211)
3 dashes of Campari
Grapefruit coin, to garnish
Thin strawberry slice, to garnish

Stir all the ingredients in a mixing
glass with ice cubes, then strain
into a chilled coupe. Express the
grapefruit coin over the top, then
discard. Garnish with a thin slice
of strawberry.

✦ Adapted by: Denis Broci, Claridge's Bar,
London

Japanese Cocktail

MAKES 1 DRINK

60ml (2fl oz) Rémy Martin VSOP
    Cognac
10ml (¼fl oz) Bristol Syrup Company
    Orgeat
3 dashes of Angostura bitters
Lemon twist, to garnish

Stir all the ingredients in a mixing
glass, then strain into a chilled coupe.
Garnish with a lemon twist.

✦ Credit: *Jerry Thomas' Bartenders Guide*
(1862)

Boulevardier

MAKES 1 DRINK

40ml (1½fl oz) Maker's Mark Bourbon
    Whisky
20ml (¾fl oz) Carpano Antica Formula
    Vermouth
20ml (¾fl oz) Campari
Orange twist, to garnish

Stir all the ingredients in a mixing
glass, then strain into a chilled coupe.
Garnish with an orange twist.

✦ Credit: Harry MacElhone, *Barflies and
Cocktails* (1927)

Bitter Orange

MAKES 1 DRINK

25ml (1fl oz) Beefeater London Dry
    Gin
15ml (½fl oz) Grand Marnier
15ml (½fl oz) Campari
15ml (½fl oz) Punt e Mes Vermouth
15ml (½fl oz) Muyu Vetiver Gris
Orange coin, to garnish

Stir all the ingredients in a mixing
glass, then strain into a chilled rocks
glass over an ice block. Garnish with
an orange coin.

✦ Credit: Denis Broci, Claridge's Bar,
London

Coffee Boulevardier

MAKES 1 DRINK

30ml (1fl oz) Michter's US*1 Kentucky
    Straight Rye Whiskey
30ml (1fl oz) Campari
15ml (½fl oz) Coffee-infused Carpano
    Antica Formula Vermouth (see
    page 203)
15ml (½fl oz) Lustau Oloroso Sherry
3 roasted coffee beans, to garnish

Stir all the ingredients in a mixing
glass, then strain into a chilled
vintage coupe. Garnish with the
coffee beans.

✦ Credit: Riccardo Semeria, The Fumoir,
London

Tuxedo

MAKES 1 DRINK

50ml (2fl oz) Tanqueray London Dry
    Gin
20ml (¾fl oz) Dolin Dry Vermouth
2 dashes of Pernod Absinthe
Lemon twist, to garnish

Stir all the ingredients in a mixing
glass, then strain into a chilled coupe.
Garnish with a lemon twist.

✦ Adapted by: Harry Craddock, The Savoy,
London

Golden Tuxedo

MAKES 1 DRINK

70ml (2½fl oz) Porter's Orchard Gin
10ml (¼fl oz) Cocchi Americano
5ml (1 tsp) Somerset Cider Brandy
2.5ml (½ tsp) Reisetbauer Karotte
    Eau de Vie
1 dash of Pernod Absinthe
Lemon twist, to garnish

Stir all the ingredients in a mixing
glass, then strain into a chilled coupe.
Garnish with a lemon twist.

✦ Credit: Alex Lawrence, Mr Lyan, London

Battle of New Orleans

MAKES 1 DRINK

60ml (2fl oz) Maker's Mark Bourbon
    Whisky
2 dashes of Pernod Absinthe
3 dashes of Peychaud's bitters
1 dash of orange bitters
Orange coin, to garnish

Stir all the ingredients in a mixing
glass, then fine-strain into a chilled
rocks glass. Express the orange coin
over the top, then discard.

Bourbon & Pear

MAKES 1 DRINK

60ml (2fl oz) Michter's US*1 Kentucky
    Straight Bourbon Whiskey
40ml (1½fl oz) Pear Cordial (see
    page 192)

Stir all the whiskey and cordial in a
mixing glass with ice cubes. Strain
into a chilled coupe.

✦ Credit: Anna Sebastian, Artesian Bar,
The Langham, London

Bushwick

MAKES 1 DRINK

50ml (2fl oz) Michter's US*1 Kentucky
    Straight Rye Whiskey
7.5ml (1½ tsp) Martini Rosso
10ml (¼fl oz) Amer Picon
7.5ml (1½ tsp) Maraschino
Fabbri Amarena cherry, to garnish

Stir all the ingredients in a mixing
glass, then strain into a chilled coupe.
Garnish with the cherry.

✦ Credit: Phil Ward, Death & Co,
New York

Drawing Board

MAKES 1 DRINK

10ml (¼fl oz) Laphroaig 10 Year Old
    Whisky
2 lemon coins
60ml (2fl oz) Glenfiddich IPA
    Experiment Whisky
15ml (½fl oz) Bénédictine
15ml (½fl oz) Drambuie
2 dashes of Jerry Thomas' Own
    Decanter Bitters

Rinse a chilled rocks glass with the
Laphroaig, then discard. Express
the lemon coins over the top of a
mixing glass, then discard. Stir in the
remaining ingredients with ice cubes,
then strain into the rocks glass over
an ice block.

✦ Credit: Jillian Vose, The Dead Rabbit,
New York

Earl of Spey

MAKES 1 DRINK

30ml (1fl oz) Glenfiddich 18 Year Old
    Whisky
25ml (1fl oz) Carpano Antica Formula
    Vermouth
5ml (1 tsp) Mr Black Cold Brew Coffee
    Liqueur
5ml (1 tsp) Fernet-Branca Menta
5ml (1 tsp) St Lawrence Gold Pure
    Maple Syrup
5 dashes of Bob's Chocolate Bitters
Orange twist, to garnish

Stir all the ingredients in a mixing
glass with ice cubes, then strain
into a chilled rocks glass over an ice
block. Garnish with an orange twist.

✦ Credit: Nathan McCarley-O'Neill,
Claridge's Bar, London

The Coley

MAKES 1 DRINK

15ml (½fl oz) Smith & Cross Jamaica
    Rum
20ml (¾fl oz) Campari
15ml (½fl oz) Carpano Antica Formula
    Vermouth
7.5ml (1½ tsp) Havana Club 3 Year Old
    Rum
7.5ml (1½ tsp) Amaro Averna
2 dashes of Bob's Chocolate Bitters
Orange twist, to garnish

Stir all the ingredients in a mixing
glass with ice cubes, then strain
into a chilled rocks glass over an ice
block. Garnish with an orange twist.

✦ Credit: Iván Villegas, Davies and Brook,
London

Corn & Oil

MAKES 1 DRINK

45ml (1½fl oz) Havana Club 7 Year Old
    Rum
15ml (½fl oz) John D Taylor's Velvet
    Falernum
2 dashes of Angostura bitters
15ml (½fl oz) Gosling's Black Seal
    Rum
Lime coin, to garnish

Stir each ingredient, except the rum,
in a mixing glass with ice cubes for
3 or 4 rotations to combine well and
chill before adding the next. Strain
into a chilled rocks glass over an ice
block, then float the rum on top.
Garnish with a lime coin.

Saint Remy

MAKES 1 DRINK

5ml (1 tsp) Cocchi Americano
5ml (1 tsp) Capreolus Quince
    Eau De Vie
5ml (1 tsp) Roger Groult 3 Year Old
    Calvados
15ml (½fl oz) Almond Blossom Cordial
    (see page 193)
35ml (1fl oz) Belvedere Vodka

Stir all the ingredients in a mixing
glass with ice cubes. Fine-strain into
a chilled Nick and Nora glass.

✦ Credit: Nathan McCarley-O'Neill,
The Painter's Room, London

→ Corn & Oil

Little Italy

MAKES 1 DRINK

50ml (2fl oz) Michter's US*1 Kentucky
    Straight Rye Whiskey
25ml (1fl oz) Martini Rosso
15ml (½fl oz) Cynar Amaro
Orange twist, to garnish

Stir all the ingredients in a mixing
glass, then strain into a chilled rocks
glass over an ice block. Garnish with
an orange twist.

✦ **Credit: Audrey Saunders, Pegu Club,
New York**

Red Hook

MAKES 1 DRINK

50ml (2fl oz) Michter's US*1 Kentucky
    Straight Rye Whiskey
12.5ml (2½ tsp) Punt e Mes Vermouth
12.5ml (2½ tsp) Maraschino
Fabbri Amarena cherry, to garnish

Stir all the ingredients in a mixing
glass with ice cubes, then strain into
a chilled coupe. Garnish with the
cherry on a cocktail stick.

✦ **Credit: Vincenzo Errico, Milk & Honey,
New York**

Cardinale

MAKES 1 DRINK

40ml (1½fl oz) Plymouth Gin
20ml (¾fl oz) Campari
15ml (½fl oz) Martini Extra Dry
    Vermouth
Lemon twist, to garnish

Stir all the ingredients in a mixing
glass, then strain into a chilled coupe.
Garnish with a lemon twist.

✦ **Credit: Luca Di Francia, Orum Bar, Rome**

Chrysanthemum

MAKES 1 DRINK

60ml (2fl oz) Lillet Blanc
10ml (¼fl oz) Bénédictine
2 dashes of Peychaud's bitters
1 dash of Pernod Absinthe
Lemon twist, to garnish

Stir all the ingredients in a mixing
glass, then strain into a chilled coupe.
Garnish with a lemon twist.

✦ **Credit: Harry Craddock, The Savoy,
London**

Stinger

MAKES 1 DRINK

50ml (2fl oz) Seven Tails XO Brandy
20ml (¾fl oz) Briottet Liqueur de
    Menthe Blanche

Stir the brandy and liqueur in a
mixing glass. Strain into a chilled
coupe.

Treacle

50ml (2fl oz) Ron Zacapa 23
    Centenario
20ml (¾fl oz) Eager Apple Juice
10ml (¼fl oz) sugar syrup (see page 21)
2 dashes of Angostura bitters
Lemon twist, to garnish

Stir all the ingredients in a mixing
glass, then strain into a chilled rocks
glass over an ice block. Garnish with
a lemon twist.

✦ Credit: Dick Bradsell

Floral Panky

40ml (1½fl oz) Rose-infused
    Plymouth Gin (see page 205)
40ml (1½fl oz) Cocchi Rosa
3 dashes of Fernet-Branca
Orange coin, to garnish

Stir all the ingredients in a mixing
glass, then strain into a chilled coupe.
Garnish with an orange coin.

✦ Credit: Michele Ridolfi, Claridge's Bar,
London

The Real McCoy

25ml (1fl oz) Beefeater London
    Garden Gin
25ml (1fl oz) Blackdown Silver Birch
    Vermouth
25ml (1fl oz) Douglas Fir-infused
    Campari (see page 203)
5ml (1 tsp) Merlet Crème de Mûre
3 dashes of Saline Solution (see
    page 210)
Blood orange slice, to garnish

Stir all the ingredients in a mixing
glass, then strain into a chilled rocks
glass over an ice block. Garnish with
a slice of blood orange.

✦ Adapted by: Nathan McCarley-O'Neill,
Dandelyan, London

Rusty Nail

40ml (1½fl oz) Johnnie Walker Black
    Label Whisky
20ml (¾fl oz) Drambuie
Lemon twist, to garnish

Stir all the whisky and Drambuie in a
mixing glass, then strain into a chilled
rocks glass. Garnish with a lemon
twist.

Short
&
Sharp

← Grasshopper (see page 111)

Pineapple Daiquiri

MAKES 1 DRINK

25ml (1fl oz) Bacardí Ron Superior
  Heritage Limited Edition
25ml (1fl oz) Plantation Stiggins'
  Fancy Pineapple Rum
25ml (1fl oz) pineapple juice
15ml (½fl oz) sugar syrup (see page 21)
15ml (½fl oz) lime juice

In a cocktail shaker, shake all the
ingredients with a large block of ice,
as well as ice cubes, until the large
block is completely broken down and
the shaker is frosted over. Fine-strain
into a chilled coupe.

✦ Adapted by: Nathan McCarley-O'Neill,
The Fumoir, London

Hemingway Daiquiri

MAKES 1 DRINK

45ml (1½fl oz) Havana Club 3 Year
  Old Rum
5ml (1 tsp) Maraschino
15ml (½fl oz) grapefruit juice
15ml (½fl oz) sugar syrup (see page 21)
10ml (¼fl oz) lime juice
Grapefruit coin, to garnish

In a cocktail shaker, shake all the
ingredients with ice cubes until very
cold, then fine-strain into a chilled
coupe. Express the grapefruit coin
over the top, then discard.

Maid

MAKES 1 DRINK

50ml (2fl oz) Tanqueray London
  Dry Gin
20ml (¾fl oz) lime juice
20ml (¾fl oz) sugar syrup (see
  page 21)
5 mint leaves
Cucumber coin, to garnish

In a cocktail shaker, shake all the
ingredients with ice cubes, then
fine-strain into a chilled rocks glass
over an ice block. Garnish with a
cucumber coin.

✦ Credit: Sam Ross, Milk & Honey, New York

Dry Daiquiri

MAKES 1 DRINK

50ml (2fl oz) Havana Club 3 Year Old
  Rum
5ml (1 tsp) Campari
15ml (½fl oz) lime juice
15ml (½fl oz) sugar syrup (see page 21)

In a cocktail shaker, shake all the
ingredients with ice cubes. Fine-
strain into a chilled coupe.

✦ Credit: Kevin Armstrong, Match Bar
Group, London

Daiquiri

MAKES 1 DRINK

50ml (2fl oz) Bacardí Ron Superior
  Heritage Limited Edition
20ml (¾fl oz) lime juice
15ml (½fl oz) sugar syrup (see page 21)

In a cocktail shaker, shake all the
ingredients with ice cubes until very
cold. Fine-strain into a chilled coupe.

✦ Credit: Jennings Cox, Cuba

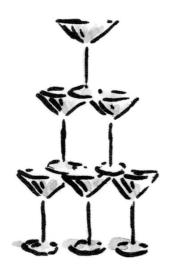

➜ Pineapple Daiquiri

Chocolate Marquisa

MAKES 1 DRINK

50ml (2fl oz) Diplomático Reserva
Exclusiva Rum
10ml (¼fl oz) Grand Marnier
5ml (1 tsp) Mozart Chocolate Liqueur
5ml (1 tsp) Monin Chocolate Syrup
20ml (¾fl oz) fresh strong espresso
Vanilla Cream (see page 212), to top up

Combine all the ingredients, except
the vanilla cream, in a saucepan and
heat gently. When warm, pour into an
Irish coffee glass and float the vanilla
cream on top.

✦ Credit: Maddalena Sommo, Hakkasan,
London

Espresso Martiki

MAKES 1 DRINK

40ml (1½fl oz) Plantation Stiggins'
Fancy Pineapple Rum
30ml (1fl oz) Mr Black Cold Brew
Coffee Liqueur
30ml (1fl oz) pineapple juice
30ml (1fl oz) fresh espresso
15ml (½fl oz) Bristol Syrup Company
Orgeat
Edible flowers, to garnish

In a cocktail shaker, shake all the
ingredients with ice cubes, then fine-
strain into a chilled coupe. Garnish
with edible flowers.

✦ Credit: Martin Hudak, Maybe Sammy,
Sydney

The Redemption

MAKES 1 DRINK

50ml (2fl oz) Havana Club Selección
de Maestros Rum
15ml (½fl oz) Lustau Pedro Ximénez
Sherry
25ml (1fl oz) Lemongrass Syrup (see
page 196)
15ml (½fl oz) lime juice

In a cocktail shaker, shake all the
ingredients with ice cubes. Fine-
strain into a chilled coupe.

✦ Credit: Elżbieta Baj, The Fumoir, London

Atlantic Nights

MAKES 1 DRINK

45ml (1½fl oz) Havana Club Especial
Rum
5ml (1 tsp) Yellow Chartreuse
5ml (1 tsp) Pernod Absinthe
15ml (½fl oz) lemon juice
12.5ml (2½ tsp) heather honey
Grapefruit coin, to garnish

In a cocktail shaker, shake all the
ingredients with ice cubes. Fine-
strain into a chilled coupe and
garnish with a grapefruit coin.

✦ Adapted by: Nathan McCarley-O'Neill,
The Fumoir, London

Pineapple Fix

MAKES 1 DRINK

50ml (2fl oz) Havana Club Especial
Rum
10ml (¼fl oz) pineapple juice
10ml (¼fl oz) lemon juice
10ml (¼fl oz) sugar syrup (see page 21)
3 fresh pineapple chunks, plus a
pineapple slice, to garnish

In a cocktail shaker, shake all the
ingredients with ice cubes, then fine-
strain into a chilled rocks glass over
an ice block. Garnish with a slice of
pineapple.

East 8 Hold Up

MAKES 1 DRINK

40ml (1½fl oz) Ketel One Vodka
15ml (½fl oz) Aperol
25ml (1fl oz) pineapple juice
15ml (½fl oz) lime juice
15ml (½fl oz) sugar syrup (see page 21)
5ml (1 tsp) passionfruit syrup
Lime wedge, to garnish

In a cocktail shaker, shake all the
ingredients with ice cubes, then
strain into a chilled large rocks glass
over an ice block. Garnish with a lime
wedge.

✦ Credit: Kevin Armstrong, Milk & Honey,
London

Artist's Special

MAKES 1 DRINK

50ml (2fl oz) Chivas Regal 12 Year Old
   Blended Scotch Whisky
10ml (¼fl oz) Lustau Pedro Ximénez
   Sherry
20ml (¾fl oz) lemon juice
10ml (¼fl oz) sugar syrup (see page 21)
6 redcurrants

In a cocktail shaker, shake all the
ingredients with ice cubes. Fine-
strain into a chilled Nick & Nora
glass.

✦ Credit: Harry MacElhone, *Barflies and
Cocktails* (1927)

Between the Sheets

MAKES 1 DRINK

35ml (1fl oz) Rémy Martin VSOP
   Cognac
15ml (½fl oz) Bénédictine
15ml (½fl oz) Cointreau
20ml (¾fl oz) lemon juice
Lemon twist, to garnish

In a cocktail shaker, shake all the
ingredients with ice cubes, then fine-
strain into a chilled coupe. Garnish
with a lemon twist.

✦ Credit: Harry MacElhone, Harry's Bar,
Paris

21st-Century Artist

MAKES 1 DRINK

30ml (1fl oz) Rémy Martin VSOP
   Cognac
10ml (¼fl oz) Adrien Camut 6 Year Old
   Calvados
15ml (½fl oz) Miclo Poire Williams Eau
   de Vie
7.5ml (1½ tsp) St-Germain elderflower
   liqueur, plus an extra spray, to
   garnish
20ml (¾fl oz) lemon juice
10ml (¼fl oz) St Lawrence Gold Pure
   Maple Syrup
1 dash of Pernod Absinthe

In a cocktail shaker, shake all the
ingredients with ice cubes, then fine-
strain into a chilled coupe. Garnish
with a spray of the elderflower
liqueur, using an atomizer.

✦ Credit: Nathan McCarley-O'Neill,
Claridge's Bar, London

Business

MAKES 1 DRINK

50ml (2fl oz) Beefeater London Dry
   Gin
20ml (¾fl oz) lime juice
20ml (¾fl oz) Heather Honey Syrup
   (see page 194)

In a cocktail shaker, shake all the
ingredients with ice cubes. Fine-
strain into a chilled coupe.

✦ Credit: Sasha Petraske, Milk & Honey,
New York

London Calling

MAKES 1 DRINK

50ml (2fl oz) Beefeater London Dry
   Gin
10ml (¼fl oz) Lustau Fino Sherry
15ml (½fl oz) lemon juice
15ml (½fl oz) sugar syrup (see page 21)
2 dashes of orange bitters
Grapefruit twist, to garnish

In a cocktail shaker, shake all the
ingredients with ice cubes, then fine-
strain into a chilled coupe. Garnish
with a grapefruit twist.

✦ Credit: Chris Jepson, Milk & Honey,
London

Silver Bullet

MAKES 1 DRINK

45ml (1½fl oz) Plymouth Gin
15ml (½fl oz) Wolfschmidt Kummel
20ml (¾fl oz) lemon juice
10ml (¼fl oz) sugar syrup (see page 21)

In a cocktail shaker, shake all the ingredients with ice cubes. Fine-strain into a chilled coupe.

French Pearl

MAKES 1 DRINK

50ml (2fl oz) Plymouth Gin
20ml (¾fl oz) lime juice
20ml (¾fl oz) sugar syrup (see page 21)
2 dashes of Pernod Absinthe
4 mint leaves

In a cocktail shaker, shake all the ingredients with ice cubes. Fine-strain into a chilled coupe.

✦ Credit: Audrey Saunders, Pegu Club, New York

Smoky Dream

MAKES 1 DRINK

40ml (1½fl oz) Tapatio Blanco Tequila
10ml (¼fl oz) Ilegal Mezcal
25ml (1fl oz) Watermelon Cordial (see page 193)
15ml (½fl oz) lime juice

In a cocktail shaker, shake all the ingredients with ice cubes. Fine-strain into a chilled rocks glass over an ice block.

✦ Credit: Alice Taraschi, The Fumoir, London

Devil's Share

MAKES 1 DRINK

50ml (2fl oz) Maker's Mark Bourbon Whisky
10ml (¼fl oz) Ginger Syrup (see page 195)
10ml (¼fl oz) St Lawrence Gold Pure Maple Syrup
20ml (¾fl oz) lemon juice
1 dash of Angostura bitters
2 orange slices, plus an orange twist, to garnish

In a cocktail shaker, shake all the ingredients with ice cubes, then fine-strain into a chilled rocks glass over an ice block. Garnish with an orange twist.

✦ Credit: Pete Kendall, Match Bar, London

Cosmopolitan

MAKES 1 DRINK

35ml (1fl oz) Ketel One Vodka
20ml (¾fl oz) Cointreau
20ml (¾fl oz) Ocean Spray Cranberry Juice
10ml (¼fl oz) lime juice
Orange coin, to garnish

In a cocktail shaker, shake all the ingredients with ice cubes, then fine-strain into a chilled coupe. Garnish with an orange coin.

✦ Credit: Toby Cecchini, The Odeon, New York

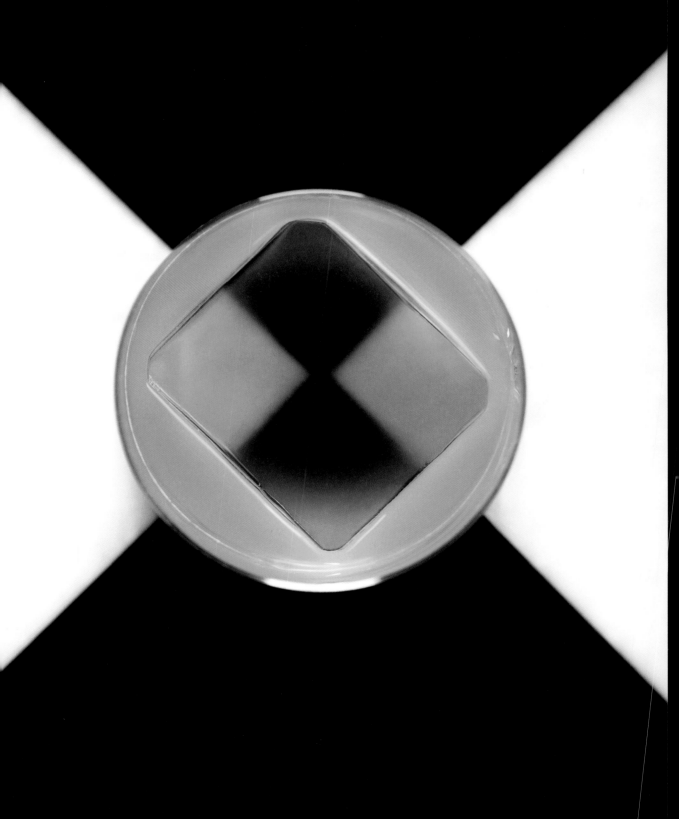

The Peruvian

MAKES 1 DRINK

40ml (1½fl oz) Barsol Pisco
20ml (¾fl oz) lime juice
15ml (½fl oz) Ginger Syrup (see page 195)
15ml (½fl oz) St Lawrence Gold Pure Maple Syrup
10ml (¼fl oz) Fernet-Branca
5 dashes of Angostura bitters
2 cucumber coins
Fever-Tree Ginger Ale, to top up
Mint sprig, to garnish
Crystallized ginger, to garnish

In a cocktail shaker, dry shake all the ingredients, except the ginger ale, then add ice cubes and shake again. Fine-strain into a chilled rocks glass over an ice block and top up with the ginger ale. Garnish with a mint sprig and a piece of crystallized ginger on a cocktail stick.

✦ Credit: Andreas Cortes, Claridge's Bar, London

Great Fitzgerald

MAKES 1 DRINK

40ml (1½fl oz) The Lakes The One Fine Blended Whisky
10ml (¼fl oz) Lustau Oloroso Sherry
5ml (1 tsp) Amer Picon
15ml (½fl oz) lemon juice
15ml (½fl oz) sugar syrup (see page 21)
1 dash of Pernod Absinthe
Orange coin, to garnish

In a cocktail shaker, shake all the ingredients with ice cubes, then fine-strain into a chilled coupe. Express the orange coin over the top, then discard.

✦ Adapted by: Nathan McCarley-O'Neill, Claridge's Bar, London

Last Word

MAKES 1 DRINK

20ml (¾fl oz) Beefeater London Dry Gin
20ml (¾fl oz) Green Chartreuse
20ml (¾fl oz) Maraschino
20ml (¾fl oz) lime juice
Fabbri Amarena cherry, to garnish

In a cocktail shaker, shake all the ingredients with ice cubes, then fine-strain into a chilled coupe. Garnish with the cherry.

✦ Credit: Ted Saucier, *Bottoms Up* (1951)

National

MAKES 1 DRINK

45ml (1½fl oz) Bacardí Carta Blanca Rum
15ml (½fl oz) Briottet Crème d'Abricot
20ml (¾fl oz) lime juice
7.5ml (1½ tsp) sugar syrup (see page 21)

In a cocktail shaker, shake all the ingredients with ice cubes. Fine-strain into a chilled coupe.

Grenoble Flip

MAKES 1 DRINK

25ml (1fl oz) Green Chartreuse
25ml (1fl oz) Maraschino
1 whole egg
Grated nutmeg, to garnish

In a cocktail shaker, dry shake all the ingredients, then add ice cubes and shake again. Fine-strain into a chilled coupe and garnish with grated nutmeg.

Jack Rose

MAKES 1 DRINK

45ml (1½fl oz) Adrien Camut 6 Year
    Old Calvados
20ml (¾fl oz) lemon juice
10ml (¼fl oz) sugar syrup (see page 21)
12.5ml (2½ tsp) Bristol Syrup
    Company Grenadine

In a cocktail shaker, shake all the
ingredients with ice cubes. Fine-
strain into a chilled coupe.

✦ Credit: Jacques Straub, *Straub's Manual
of Mixed Drinks* (1913)

Basis for Theory

MAKES 1 DRINK

35ml (1fl oz) Ocho Tequila
20ml (¾fl oz) Tarragon-infused Dolin
    Dry Vermouth (see page 207)
15ml (½fl oz) sugar syrup (see page 21)
15ml (½fl oz) lemon juice
5ml (1 tsp) Empirical Habanero Spirit
1 dash of Pernod Absinthe
3 tarragon leaves, to garnish

In a cocktail shaker, shake all the
ingredients with ice cubes, then fine-
strain into a chilled rocks glass over
an ice block. Garnish with 3 tarragon
leaves on top of the ice block.

✦ Adapted by: Nathan McCarley-O'Neill,
Claridge's Bar, London

Nostalgia

MAKES 1 DRINK

Pink Himalayan salt
75ml (2½fl oz) Graham's Blend No 5
    White Port
35ml (1fl oz) Lacto-fermented
    Blueberry Wine (see page 213)
5ml (1 tsp) Pineapple Saccharum (see
    page 213)

Half-rim a chilled wine glass with
Pink Himalayan salt (see page 19).
In a cocktail shaker, shake all the
ingredients with ice cubes, then
strain into the glass over ice cubes.

✦ Credit: Raffaele Di Monaco, Blue Bar,
The Berkeley, London

Savoy Daisy

MAKES 1 DRINK

60ml (2fl oz) Graham's Fine Ruby Port
20ml (¾fl oz) Bacardí 8 Year Old Rum
10ml (¼fl oz) Diplomático Reserva
    Exclusiva Rum
30ml (1fl oz) lime juice
15ml (½fl oz) Bristol Syrup Company
    Grenadine
1 bar spoon muscovado sugar
Orange twist, to garnish.

In a cocktail shaker, shake all the
ingredients with ice cubes, then fine-
strain into a chilled coupe. Garnish
with an orange twist.

✦ Credit: Daniel Baernreuther, The Savoy,
London

Caipirinha

MAKES 1 DRINK

6 lime wedges, plus an extra wedge, to
    garnish
20ml (¾fl oz) sugar syrup (see
    page 21)
50ml (2fl oz) Avuá Prata Cachaça

Muddle the lime wedges and sugar
syrup in a chilled rocks glass. Add
the cachaça and some crushed
ice and churn. Top up with more
crushed ice and garnish with another
lime wedge.

Caipiroska

MAKES 1 DRINK

6 lime wedges, plus an extra wedge, to
    garnish
20ml (¾fl oz) sugar syrup (see
    page 21)
50ml (2fl oz) Ketel One Vodka

Muddle the lime wedges and sugar
syrup in a chilled rocks glass. Add
the vodka and some crushed ice and
churn. Top up with more
crushed ice and garnish with
another lime wedge.

Black Pearl

MAKES 1 DRINK

20ml (¾fl oz) Zubrówka Bison Grass
    Vodka
10ml (¼fl oz) Botanist Islay Dry Gin
10ml (¼fl oz) Chambord
15ml (½fl oz) Briottet Crème de Cassis
50ml (2fl oz) pink grapefruit juice
20ml (¾fl oz) lemon juice
6 blueberries
3 blackberries, plus an extra
    blackberry, halved, to garnish

In a cocktail shaker, shake all the
ingredients with ice cubes, then
fine-strain into a chilled rocks glass
over an ice block. Garnish with a
halved blackberry placed carefully
on top of the ice.

✦ Credit: Jorge Oliveira, Claridge's Bar,
London

Bramble

MAKES 1 DRINK

40ml (1½fl oz) Bombay Sapphire Gin
20ml (¾fl oz) lemon juice
7.5ml (1½ tsp) sugar syrup (see
    page 21)
10ml (¼fl oz) Briottet Crème de Mûre
Lemon wedge, to garnish
Blackberry, to garnish

Build the ingredients, except the
crème de mûre, in a chilled rocks
glass. Add crushed ice and float the
crème de mûre on top of the drink.
Garnish with a lemon wedge and a
blackberry.

✦ Credit: Dick Bradsell, Fred's Club, London

H S L Special

MAKES 1 DRINK

35ml (1fl oz) Amaro Montenegro
15ml (½fl oz) Merlet Crème de Mûre
25ml (1fl oz) lime juice
7.5ml (1½ tsp) sugar syrup (see
    page 21)
1 dash of Pernod Absinthe
Blackberry, to garnish
Icing sugar, to garnish

In a cocktail shaker, shake all the
ingredients with ice cubes, then
fine-strain into a chilled rocks
glass over an ice block. Garnish
with a blackberry and a sprinkling
of icing sugar.

✦ Credit: Hayden Scott Lambert,
Above Board, Melbourne

Southside

MAKES 1 DRINK

50ml (2fl oz) Plymouth Gin
20ml (¾fl oz) lime juice
20ml (¾fl oz) sugar syrup (see
    page 21)
4 mint leaves

In a cocktail shaker, shake all
the ingredients with ice cubes.
Fine-strain into a chilled coupe.

Pineapple Punch

MAKES 1 DRINK

30ml (1fl oz) Rémy Martin XO Cognac
30ml (1fl oz) Plantation Stiggins'
    Fancy Pineapple Rum
10ml (¼fl oz) Green Chartreuse
35ml (1fl oz) Eager Pineapple Juice
20ml (¾fl oz) Winter Syrup (see
    page 197)
20ml (¾fl oz) milk
15ml (½fl oz) chai tea
5ml (1 tsp) lemon juice
Grated nutmeg, to garnish

Mix all the ingredients in a mixing glass and rest for 13 minutes. Once the drink starts curdling, strain through a paper coffee filter (make sure you rinse the coffee filter before using).

Serve immediately in a chilled large rocks glass, garnished with grated nutmeg, or keep in the refrigerator if you are making a larger quantity to serve to friends.

✦ **Inspired by: Christian Louboutin's Claridge's Christmas Tree 2019 Credit: Denis Broci, Claridge's Bar, London**

A Farewell to Arms

MAKES 1 DRINK

45ml (1½fl oz) Bacardí Carta Blanca
    Rum
15ml (½fl oz) Italicus Rosolio Di
    Bergamotto
10ml (¼fl oz) Ginger Syrup (see
    page 195)
10ml (¼fl oz) Heather Honey Syrup
    (see page 194)
20ml (¾fl oz) lime juice
5ml (1 tsp) orange juice
5ml (1 tsp) sugar syrup (see page 21)
Grapefruit coin, to garnish

In a cocktail shaker, shake all the ingredients with ice cubes, then fine-strain into a chilled coupe. Garnish with a grapefruit coin.

✦ **Credit: Riccardo Semeria, The Fumoir, London**

Hotel Nacional

MAKES 1 DRINK

40ml (1½fl oz) Havana Club 3 Year
    Old Rum
20ml (¾fl oz) pineapple juice
15ml (½fl oz) lime juice
10ml (¼fl oz) sugar syrup (see page 21)
5ml (1 tsp) Merlet Lune d'Abricot
1 dash of Pernod Absinthe
1 dash of Angostura bitters

In a cocktail shaker, shake all the ingredients with ice cubes until very cold. Fine-strain into a chilled coupe.

Cloud of Mists

MAKES 1 DRINK

35ml (1fl oz) Roku Gin
15ml (½fl oz) Gyokuro-infused
    Darroze 8 Year Old Armagnac
    (see page 204)
15ml (½fl oz) Aperitivo Del Professore
30ml (1fl oz) Mandarin Shrub (see
    page 191)
1 peach from a bag of Abukuma Baby
    Peach Compote, to garnish

In a cocktail shaker, shake all the ingredients with ice cubes, then fine-strain into a chilled coupe. Garnish with an Abukuma Baby Peach.

✦ **Credit: Mehdi Ichedadene, Coburg Bar, Connaught Hotel, London**

Paper Plane

MAKES 1 DRINK

20ml (¾fl oz) Maker's Mark Bourbon
    Whisky
20ml (¾fl oz) Amaro Nonino
20ml (¾fl oz) Aperol
20ml (¾fl oz) lemon juice

In a cocktail shaker, shake all the ingredients with ice cubes. Fine-strain into a chilled coupe.

✦ **Credit: Sam Ross, The Violet Hour, Chicago**

Pirate Queen

MAKES 1 DRINK

30ml (1fl oz) Plantation Barbados
    5 Year Old Rum
20ml (¾fl oz) Bols Genever Original
30ml (1fl oz) lemon juice
15ml (½fl oz) Strawberry Syrup (see
    page 197)
7.5ml (1½ tsp) Ginger Syrup (see
    page 195)
7.5ml (1½ tsp) Heather Honey Syrup
    (see page 194)
7.5ml (1½ tsp) Cinnamon Bark Syrup
    (see page 195)
Grated nutmeg, to garnish

In a cocktail shaker, shake all the
ingredients with ice cubes, then fine-
strain into a chilled coupe. Garnish
with grated nutmeg.

✦ **Credit: Jillian Vose, The Dead Rabbit,
New York**

Eastside Cocktail

MAKES 1 DRINK

50ml (2fl oz) Plymouth Gin
20ml (¾fl oz) lime juice
15ml (½fl oz) sugar syrup (see page 21)
2 cucumber slices, plus a cucumber
    coin, to garnish
4 mint leaves

In a cocktail shaker, shake all the
ingredients with ice cubes, then fine-
strain into a chilled coupe. Garnish
with a cucumber coin.

✦ **Credit: George Delgado, Libation,
New York**

Fitzgerald

MAKES 1 DRINK

50ml (2fl oz) Beefeater London Dry
    Gin
15ml (½fl oz) lemon juice
15ml (½fl oz) sugar syrup (see page 21)
2 dashes of Angostura bitters

In a cocktail shaker, shake all the
ingredients with ice cubes. Fine-
strain into a chilled coupe.

✦ **Credit: Dale DeGroff, The Rainbow Room,
New York**

Green Park

MAKES 1 DRINK

50ml (2fl oz) Haymans Old Tom Gin
30ml (1fl oz) lemon juice
15ml (½fl oz) Cane Syrup (see page
    194)
3 dashes of Bitter Truth Celery Bitters
3 basil leaves
1 egg white

In a cocktail shaker, dry shake all the
ingredients, then add ice cubes and
shake again. Fine-strain into a chilled
coupe.

✦ **Credit: Erik Lorincz, The Savoy, London**

Corpse Reviver No 2

MAKES 1 DRINK

20ml (¾floz) Plymouth Gin
20ml (¾fl oz) Lillet Blanc
20ml (¾fl oz) Combier Triple Sec
20ml (¾fl oz) lemon juice
5ml (1 tsp) sugar syrup (see page 21)
1 dash of Pernod Absinthe
Orange coin, to garnish

In a cocktail shaker, shake all the ingredients with ice cubes, then fine-strain into a chilled coupe. Express the orange coin over the top, then discard.

✦ Credit: Harry Craddock, The Savoy, London

Fifth Avenue Daiquiri

MAKES 1 DRINK

40ml (1½fl oz) Bacardí Ron Superior Heritage Limited Edition
15ml (½fl oz) Graham's 10 Year Old Tawny Port
10ml (¼fl oz) Lustau Pedro Ximénez Sherry
15ml (½fl oz) lemon juice
1 bar spoon caster sugar
1 dash of Peychaud's Bitters

In a cocktail shaker, shake all the ingredients with ice cubes. Fine-strain into a chilled coupe.

✦ Adapted by: Nathan McCarley-O'Neill, The Fumoir, London

L'Incontro

MAKES 1 DRINK

35ml (1fl oz) Del Maguey Vida Mezcal
20ml (¾fl oz) Luxardo Maraschino Liqueur
15ml (½fl oz) Aperol
15ml (½fl oz) lemon juice
4 dashes of Legendre Herbsaint

In a cocktail shaker, shake all the ingredients with ice cubes. Fine-strain into a chilled coupe.

✦ Credit: Ezra Star, Hong Kong

Mulata Daisy

MAKES 1 DRINK

Cacao powder
½ bar spoon fennel seeds
45ml (1½fl oz) Bacardí Carta Blanca Rum
15ml (½fl oz) Briottet Crème de Cacao (Cocoa)
10ml (¼fl oz) Galliano L'Autentico
20ml (¾fl oz) lime juice
5ml (1 tsp) sugar syrup (see page 21)

Rim a chilled coupe with cacao powder (see page 19). Crush the fennel seeds in a cocktail shaker, then add the remaining ingredients. Shake with ice cubes, then fine-strain into the glass.

✦ Credit: Agostino Perrone, Connaught Bar, London

How to create a new cocktail

What is the purpose of a cocktail? To surprise? To delight? To begin the night on an upbeat note or end it on a sophisticated one? From the very first cocktail party in 1925 – when Alec Waugh and his sherbet-sweet daiquiris caught everyone off-guard (his guests had been expecting traditional tea) – cocktails have brought much to the table.

Since that date, a great many cocktails have been invented – in this book alone you will find more than 400 of them, and we have, naturally, been rather discerning. Yet most cocktails come and go. The ones that remain do so for a reason. As a prospective author might begin his journey in the library, so should a bartender-in-the-making look to great works of the past before picking up a shaker.

For those seeking inspiration, there are recipe books dating back to the late 1800s – many with cocktails you would still find on menus today – while a number of dedicated websites exist to unveil the many hard-won secrets of the trade.

At Claridge's, inspiration can be found at every turn. Bartenders swap ideas with the kitchen team, combining tasting notes, flavour combinations and themes that stretch across the hotel – a heady perfume, a sharp fruit or a spray of brightly coloured flowers flowing down the main staircase.

Of course, it is highly recommended that you make – and taste – a good selection of classic cocktails before embarking on your own creations. This will give you a sense of what flavours work with which spirits.

At Claridge's, a bartender begins a design by selecting two key ingredients, then works the rest of the ingredients around them. Seasonality is preferred: the punch at Davies and Brook, for example, changes throughout the year, from rhubarb in spring to fig in autumn. At Claridge's Bar, there are five new cocktails each month, highlighting the best produce of the season.

The next stage is to consider how best to maximize the flavours. Do the ingredients need to be cooked, juiced, distilled or infused? Of course, this is when it helps to have some of the world's best chefs just moments from the bar and the team can often be seen heading to the kitchen to seek an expert opinion.

Then it is time to see how the flavours cope when alcohol is introduced. Strong spirits can overwhelm delicate notes, but others respond pleasingly, with botanicals from the base spirit opening up or altering the ingredients in delicious new ways. Ideally, the spirit should enhance the flavours without saturating the taste. So, if you order a Green Fig Old Fashioned (see page 63) from the Claridge's menu, you can expect it to taste of green figs.

Now for the recipe. A basic cocktail rule is one part sour, one part sweet, two parts spirit. This works well in a classic drink, such as a Tom Collins or margarita. But it is common for experienced bartenders to go off-piste when it comes to new creations. As the saying goes, you must learn the rules like a pro before you can break them like an artist.

Tasting notes are recommended. Record and evaluate each measurement, mixing style, glassware and ice combination until the perfect blend is found. Make modifications one by one, to ensure each element's contribution is considered.

Drinks with denser ingredients such as juice and citrus fruits tend to be shaken. They need more force to integrate and can stand being thrown around with lots of ice. A stronger drink such as an Old Fashioned or negroni should be stirred to avoid watering it down. Decide upon the style of ice needed

before considering presentation and glassware, as one necessarily influences the other. And consider the 'life span' of a cocktail, by tasting it immediately after it has been made, then after two, five and ten minutes. Doing this reveals how the cocktail develops and whether the mixing, glassware or ice need to be adjusted.

A long drink served in a highball over cubed or crushed ice needs bolder flavours to combat dilution. A short drink served over an ice block may need to be served slightly under-diluted, so it is perfect by the time it reaches the guest. And stirred drinks served straight up require the dilution and temperature to be precisely correct upon pouring.

An element of fizz can be added with a splash of soda, tonic (which adds bitterness), ginger ale (which adds sweetness and spice) or, for a stronger sensation, a touch of Champagne or sparkling wine. Serve a Champagne cocktail in a flute or coupe: the former sends the aromatics straight to the nose, while the latter disperses them, opening up the cocktail.

Finally, garnish. A garnish should add scent or flavour – or both – rather than simply enhance the look. Favourites are citrus fruit,

berries and mint sprigs, which add freshness and enhance the aromas of the cocktail. Chocolate can also make a wonderful addition, its rich sweetness and heady scent pairing beautifully with darker spirits such as whisky or rum. On the menu at Claridge's you will find The Royal Stag (see page 68), a delicious blend of whisky, vermouth, Campari and Bénédictine, garnished with a dark square of Claridge's chocolate, the famous golden emblem drawing the eye to the centre of the glass. On occasion, more is most definitely more.

However, please don't add garnish for the sake of it. A minimalist drink, in a beautiful glass with a crystal-clear block of ice, may not need any addition. Trust your instincts.

At the end, ask yourself the most important question: is this a drink I would order again? If the answer is yes, you have succeeded.

Painkiller

MAKES 1 DRINK

40ml (1½fl oz) El Dorado 12 Year Old Rum
40ml (1½fl oz) pineapple juice
15ml (½fl oz) orange juice
12.5ml (2½ tsp) coconut cream
Orange wedge, to garnish

In a cocktail shaker, short shake all the ingredients with 3 ice cubes for 6–8 seconds, then strain into a chilled rocks glass over an ice block. Garnish with an orange wedge.

✦ Credit: Jost Van Dyke, Soggy Dollar Bar, British Virgin Islands

Five Islands

MAKES 1 DRINK

30ml (1fl oz) Star of Bombay Gin
20ml (¾fl oz) Banks 5 Island Rum
10ml (¼fl oz) Italicus Rosolio Di Bergamotto
25ml (1fl oz) Parsnip Syrup (see page 197)
25ml (1fl oz) lemon juice
1 egg white
Ground grains of paradise, to garnish

In a cocktail shaker, dry shake all the ingredients, then add ice cubes and shake again. Fine-strain into a chilled coupe. Garnish with ground grains of paradise sprinkled in the middle of the drink.

✦ Adapted by: Denis Broci, Claridge's Bar, London

Mai Tai

(Trader Vic's version)

MAKES 1 DRINK

40ml (1½fl oz) Appleton Estate Jamaica Rum
15ml (½fl oz) Combier Triple Sec
15ml (½fl oz) lime juice
10ml (¼fl oz) Bristol Syrup Company Orgeat
2 dashes of Angostura bitters

TO GARNISH
Lemon wedge
Orange wedge
Mint sprig
Fabbri Amarena cherry

In a cocktail shaker, shake all the ingredients with ice cubes, then fine-strain into a chilled rocks glass over crushed ice. Garnish with a lemon wedge, an orange wedge, a mint sprig and a cherry.

✦ Credit: Victor Bergeron, *Trader Vic's Bartender's Guide* (1947, 1972)

Mai Tai

(Donn Beach's version)

MAKES 1 DRINK

35ml (1fl oz) Appleton Estate Jamaica Rum
15ml (½fl oz) Combier Triple Sec
15ml (½fl oz) grapefruit juice
15ml (½fl oz) lime juice
10ml (¼fl oz) John D Taylor's Velvet Falernum
10ml (¼fl oz) sugar syrup (see page 21)
2 dashes of Pernod Absinthe
2 dashes of Angostura bitters
Mint sprig, to garnish
Fabbri Amarena cherry, to garnish

In a cocktail shaker, shake all the ingredients with ice cubes, then fine-strain into a chilled rocks glass over crushed ice. Garnish with a mint sprig and a cherry.

✦ Credit: Donn Beach, Don the Beachcomber, Hollywood

➙ Left to right
Mai Tai (Trader Vic's version)
Mai Tai (Donn Beach's version)

Penicillin

- **40ml (1½fl oz) Johnnie Walker Black Label Whisky**
- **20ml (¾fl oz) lemon juice**
- **10ml (¼fl oz) Ginger Syrup (see page 195)**
- **10ml (¼fl oz) Heather Honey Syrup (see page 194)**
- **10ml (¼fl oz) Laphroaig 10 Year Old Whisky**
- **Lemon wedge, to garnish**
- **Crystallized ginger, to garnish**

In a cocktail shaker, shake all the ingredients, except the Laphroaig, with ice cubes, then strain into a chilled large rocks glass over an ice block. Float the Laphroaig on top of the drink and garnish with a lemon wedge and a piece of crystallized ginger on a cocktail stick.

✦ **Credit: Sam Ross, Milk & Honey, New York**

Knickerbocker

MAKES 1 DRINK

- **40ml (1½fl oz) Havana Club Especial Rum**
- **10ml (¼fl oz) Combier Triple Sec**
- **15ml (½fl oz) lime juice**
- **15ml (½fl oz) sugar syrup (see page 21)**
- **2 raspberries, plus an extra raspberry, to garnish**
- **Lime wedge, to garnish**
- **Mint sprig, to garnish**

In a cocktail shaker, shake all the ingredients with ice cubes, then fine-strain into a chilled rocks glass filled with crushed ice. Garnish with a lime wedge, a mint sprig and a raspberry.

✦ **Credit: *Jerry Thomas' Bartenders Guide* (1862)**

New York Flip

MAKES 1 DRINK

- **25ml (1fl oz) Maker's Mark Bourbon Whisky**
- **20ml (¾fl oz) Graham's Late Bottled Vintage Port**
- **20ml (¾fl oz) double cream**
- **20ml (¾fl oz) sugar syrup (see page 21)**
- **1 whole egg**
- **Grated nutmeg, to garnish**

In a cocktail shaker, dry shake all the ingredients, then add ice cubes and shake again. Fine-strain into a chilled coupe and garnish with grated nutmeg.

Cock of the Rock

MAKES 1 DRINK

- **45ml (1½fl oz) El Dorado 15 Year Old Rum**
- **10ml (¼fl oz) Campari**
- **35ml (1fl oz) pineapple juice**
- **20ml (¾fl oz) Bristol Syrup Company Coconut**
- **5ml (1 tsp) lime juice**
- **Mint sprig, to garnish**

In a cocktail shaker, shake all the ingredients with ice cubes, then strain into a chilled rocks glass over an ice block. Garnish with a mint sprig.

Classic Jasmine Cocktail

MAKES 1 DRINK

- **45ml (1½fl oz) Plymouth Gin**
- **15ml (½fl oz) Campari**
- **7.5ml (1½ tsp) Cointreau**
- **20ml (¾fl oz) lemon juice**
- **10ml (¼fl oz) sugar syrup (see page 21)**
- **Lemon coin, to garnish**

In a cocktail shaker, shake all the ingredients with ice cubes, then fine-strain into a chilled coupe. Express the lemon coin over the top, then discard.

✦ **Credit: Paul Harrington, Emeryville, California**

Mary Pickford

MAKES 1 DRINK

40ml (1½fl oz) Bacardí Carta Blanca Rum
10ml (¼fl oz) Maraschino
25ml (1fl oz) pineapple juice
10ml (¼fl oz) lemon juice
10ml (¼fl oz) Bristol Syrup Company Grenadine
5ml (1 tsp) sugar syrup (see page 21)
Fabbri Amarena cherry, to garnish

In a cocktail shaker, shake all the ingredients with ice cubes, then fine-strain into a chilled coupe. Garnish with the cherry.

✦ Credit: Fred Kaufman, Hotel Naçional de Cuba, Havana

Lazy Man Flip

MAKES 1 DRINK

25ml (1fl oz) Adrien Camut 6 Year Old Calvados
20ml (¾fl oz) Graham's Late Bottled Vintage Port
20ml (¾fl oz) double cream
20ml (¾fl oz) sugar syrup (see page 21)
1 whole egg
Grated nutmeg, to garnish

In a cocktail shaker, dry shake all the ingredients, then add ice cubes and shake again. Fine-strain into a chilled coupe and garnish with grated nutmeg.

✦ Credit: Chris Jepson, Milk & Honey, London

Straight Flush

MAKES 1 DRINK

2 strawberries
40ml (1½fl oz) Merlet XO Cognac
15ml (½fl oz) Aperol
15ml (½fl oz) pink grapefruit juice
10ml (¼fl oz) lemon juice
20ml (¾fl oz) sugar syrup (see page 21)
Grapefruit slice, to garnish
Mint sprig, to garnish

Muddle the strawberries in a cocktail shaker, then add the remaining ingredients and shake with ice cubes. Fine-strain into a chilled rocks glass over an ice block and garnish with a grapefruit slice and a mint sprig.

✦ Credit: Joshua Joyce, Satan's Whiskers, London

Start Me Up

MAKES 1 DRINK

30ml (1fl oz) Elijah Craig Bourbon Whiskey
15ml (½fl oz) Mount Gay Black Barrel Rum
15ml (½fl oz) Liquore Strega
7.5ml (1½ tsp) Heather Honey Syrup (see page 194)
7.5ml (1½ tsp) Ginger Syrup (see page 195)
4 dashes of orange bitters

In a cocktail shaker, shake all the ingredients with ice cubes. Fine-strain into a chilled rocks glass over an ice block.

✦ Credit: Leo Robitschek, NoMad Hotel, New York

Café Espresso

(Davies and Brook)

MAKES 1 DRINK

90ml (3fl oz) Café Espresso Batch (see page 201)

Coffee bean, to garnish

Pour the espresso batch into a chilled rocks glass over an ice block and stir for 8 to 10 rotations. Grate a single coffee bean over the ice block, to garnish.

✦ **Credit: Matteo Carretta**

Monkey Gland

MAKES 1 DRINK

40ml (1½fl oz) Plymouth Gin
30ml (1fl oz) orange juice
10ml (¼fl oz) lemon juice
10ml (¼fl oz) sugar syrup (see page 21)
5ml (1 tsp) Bristol Syrup Company Grenadine
2 dashes of Pernod Absinthe
Orange coin, to garnish

In a cocktail shaker, shake all the ingredients with ice cubes, then fine-strain into a chilled coupe. Garnish with an orange coin.

✦ **Credit: Harry MacElhone,** *Harry's ABC of Mixing Cocktails* **(1923)**

Mitch Martini

MAKES 1 DRINK

45ml (1½fl oz) Zubrówka Bison Grass Vodka
5ml (1 tsp) Briottet Crème de Pêche
20ml (¾fl oz) Eager Apple Juice
5ml (1 tsp) Bristol Syrup Company Passionfruit
Lemon twist, to garnish

In a cocktail shaker, shake all the ingredients with ice cubes, then fine-strain into a chilled coupe. Garnish with a lemon twist.

✦ **Credit: Giovanni Burdi, Match EC1, London**

Espresso Martini

MAKES 1 DRINK

40ml (1½fl oz) Grey Goose Vodka
12.5ml (2½ tsp) Mr Black Cold Brew Coffee Liqueur
25ml (1fl oz) fresh espresso
10ml (¼fl oz) sugar syrup (see page 21)
3 coffee beans, to garnish

In a cocktail shaker, shake all the ingredients with ice cubes, then fine-strain into a chilled coupe. Garnish with 3 coffee beans.

✦ **Credit: Dick Bradsell, Fred's Club, London**

French Martini

MAKES 1 DRINK

40ml (1½fl oz) Ketel One Vodka
25ml (1fl oz) Chambord
40ml (1½fl oz) pineapple juice

In a cocktail shaker, shake all the ingredients with ice cubes. Fine-strain into a chilled coupe.

Passionfruit Martini

MAKES 1 DRINK

50ml (2fl oz) Belvedere Vodka
10ml (¼fl oz) Bristol Syrup Company Passionfruit
5ml (1 tsp) sugar syrup (see page 21)
20ml (¾fl oz) lemon juice
½ a passionfruit, to garnish

In a cocktail shaker, shake all the ingredients with ice cubes, then fine-strain into a chilled coupe. Garnish with the passionfruit.

→ Café Espresso

Bitter Reviver

MAKES 1 DRINK

40ml (1½fl oz) Hepple Gin
12.5ml (2½ tsp) Combier Triple Sec
10ml (¼fl oz) Yellow Chartreuse
15ml (½fl oz) lemon juice
5ml (1 tsp) sugar syrup (see page 21)
2 dashes of orange flower water
Lemon coin, to garnish

In a cocktail shaker, shake all the ingredients with ice cubes, then fine-strain into a chilled coupe. Garnish with a lemon coin.

✦ **Credit: Denis Broci, Claridge's Bar, London**

Breakfast Martini

MAKES 1 DRINK

50ml (2fl oz) Beefeater London Dry Gin
15ml (½fl oz) Cointreau
15ml (½fl oz) lemon juice
1 tbsp orange marmalade
Orange coin, to garnish

In a cocktail shaker, shake all the ingredients with ice cubes, then fine-strain into a chilled coupe. Express the orange coin over the top, then discard.

✦ **Credit: Salvatore Calabrese**

Pineapple Martini

MAKES 1 DRINK

50ml (2fl oz) Grey Goose Vodka
40ml (1½fl oz) pineapple juice
15ml (½fl oz) lime juice
7.5ml (1½ tsp) sugar syrup (see page 21)
Pineapple wedge, to garnish

In a cocktail shaker, shake all the ingredients with ice cubes, then fine-strain into a chilled coupe. Garnish with a pineapple wedge on the rim of the glass.

✦ **Credit: Ben Reed, Met Bar, London**

Burrough's Reviver

MAKES 1 DRINK

40ml (1½fl oz) Beefeater 24 Gin
20ml (¾fl oz) Svöl Danish-Style Aquavit
15ml (½fl oz) Bristol Syrup Company Orgeat
15ml (½fl oz) lemon juice
2.5ml (½ tsp) sugar syrup (see page 21)
2 dashes of Pernod Absinthe

In a cocktail shaker, shake all the ingredients with ice cubes. Fine-strain into a chilled coupe.

✦ **Credit: Nathan McCarley-O'Neill, Merchant Hotel, Belfast**

Troigros Sour

MAKES 1 DRINK

1 egg white
5ml (1 tsp) lemon juice
5ml (1 tsp) Muyu Jasmine Verte
10ml (¼fl oz) Graham's Fine White Port
15ml (½fl oz) sorrel juice (this will need to be made with fresh sorrel using a juicer)
15ml (½fl oz) celery juice
30ml (1fl oz) Tapatio Blanco Tequila
Grated wasabi pea, to garnish

In a cocktail shaker, shake all the ingredients with ice cubes. Fine strain into a chilled coupe and garnish with a grated wasabi pea.

✦ **Credit: Nathan McCarley-O'Neill, The Painter's Room, London**

→ Bitter Reviver

Irish Coffee

50ml (2fl oz) Redbreast 12 Year Old
    Whiskey
125ml (4fl oz) filter coffee
15ml (½fl oz) demerara sugar
50ml (2fl oz) double cream
Grated nutmeg, to garnish

Fill an Irish coffee glass with freshly
boiled water to warm. Empty the
water out and build the ingredients,
except the double cream, into the
hot glass. Whip the double cream
to thicken it slightly, then float the
cream on top and garnish with
grated nutmeg.

Army & Navy

MAKES 1 DRINK

50ml (2fl oz) Plymouth Gin
15ml (½fl oz) Bristol Syrup Company
    Orgeat
15ml (½fl oz) lemon juice
5ml (1 tsp) sugar syrup (see page 21)

In a cocktail shaker, shake all the
ingredients with ice cubes. Fine-
strain into a chilled coupe.

✦ **Credit:** David A Embury, *The Fine Art of
Mixing Drinks* (1948)

Hot Chocolate #1

MAKES 1 DRINK

25ml (1fl oz) Miclo Kirsch Tradition
    Eau de Vie
15ml (½fl oz) Mr Black Cold Brew
    Coffee Liqueur
125ml (4fl oz) Hot Chocolate (see
    page 215)
30ml (1fl oz) double cream
Grated tonka bean, to garnish

Fill a coffee glass with freshly boiled
water to warm. Empty the water out
and build the ingredients, except the
double cream, in the hot glass. Float
the cream on top and garnish with
grated tonka bean.

Coffee Cocktail

MAKES 1 DRINK

30ml (1fl oz) Rémy Martin VSOP
    Cognac
30ml (1fl oz) Graham's Late Bottled
    Vintage Port
15ml (½fl oz) sugar syrup (see page 21)
1 egg
Grated nutmeg, to garnish

In a cocktail shaker, dry shake all the
ingredients, then add ice cubes and
shake again. Fine-strain into a chilled
coupe and garnish with grated
nutmeg.

✦ **Credit:** *Jerry Thomas' Bartenders Guide*
(1862)

➙ **Coffee Cocktail**

Delicious Sour

MAKES 1 DRINK

40ml (1½fl oz) Adrien Camut 6 Year
    Old Calvados
10ml (¼fl oz) Merlet Crème de Pêche
20ml (¾fl oz) lemon juice
15ml (½fl oz) sugar syrup (see page 21)
1 egg white

In a cocktail shaker, dry shake all the
ingredients, then add ice cubes and
shake again. Fine-strain into a chilled
coupe.

✦ **Credit: William Schmidt,** *The Flowing
Bowl* **(1892)**

Trinidad Sour

MAKES 1 DRINK

25ml (1fl oz) Angostura bitters
20ml (¾fl oz) Michter's US*1
    Kentucky Straight Rye Whiskey
20ml (¾fl oz) lemon juice
30ml (1fl oz) Bristol Syrup Company
    Orgeat

In a cocktail shaker, shake all the
ingredients with ice cubes. Fine-
strain into a chilled coupe.

✦ **Credit: Giuseppe González, Clover Club,
New York**

Barnard Sour

MAKES 1 DRINK

50ml (2fl oz) Barnard Batch (see
    page 201)
15ml (½fl oz) lemon juice
10ml (¼fl oz) Heather Honey Syrup
    (see page 194)
10ml (¼fl oz) Ginger Syrup (see
    page 195)
10ml (¼fl oz) Capreolus Perry Pear
    Eau de Vie
5ml (1 tsp) Kamm & Sons

In a cocktail shaker, shake all
the ingredients with ice cubes.
Fine-strain into a chilled rocks
glass over an ice block.

✦ **Credit: Nathan McCarley-O'Neill,
The Painter's Room, London**

Almond Flower Sour

MAKES 1 DRINK

30ml (1fl oz) Beefeater London Dry
    Gin
20ml (¾fl oz) lemon juice
15ml (½fl oz) Almond Flower Syrup
    (see page 195)
15ml (½fl oz) egg white
Lemon twist, to garnish

In a cocktail shaker, dry shake all the
ingredients, then shake again with
ice cubes. Fine-strain into a chilled
coupe and garnish with a lemon
twist.

✦ **Credit: Noel Venning, Three Sheets,
London**

New York Sour

MAKES 1 DRINK

40ml (1½fl oz) Maker's Mark Bourbon
    Whisky
10ml (¼fl oz) Cocchi Barolo Chinato
20ml (¾fl oz) lemon juice
20ml (¾fl oz) sugar syrup (see
    page 21)
1 egg white

In a cocktail shaker, dry shake all the
ingredients, then add ice cubes and
shake again. Fine-strain into a chilled
coupe.

→ Delicious Sour

Burlington Sour

MAKES 1 DRINK

40ml (1½fl oz) Johnnie Walker Black
    Label Whisky
10ml (¼fl oz) Cocchi Barolo Chinato
5ml (1 tsp) RinQuinQuin à la Pêche
15g (½ oz) caster sugar
15ml (½fl oz) lemon juice
1 egg white
3 drops of Peychaud's bitters, to
    garnish

In a cocktail shaker, dry shake all the
ingredients, then add ice cubes and
shake again. Fine-strain into a chilled
coupe and garnish with 3 drops of
Peychaud's bitters.

B&B Sour

MAKES 1 DRINK

35ml (1fl oz) Rémy Martin VSOP
    Cognac
15ml (½fl oz) Bénédictine
20ml (¾fl oz) lemon juice
15ml (½fl oz) sugar syrup (see page 21)
1 egg white
Orange slice, to garnish

In a cocktail shaker, dry shake all the
ingredients, then add ice cubes and
shake again. Fine-strain into a chilled
rocks glass over an ice block. Garnish
with a slice of orange.

Amaretto Sour

MAKES 1 DRINK

35ml (1fl oz) Disaronno Amaretto
20ml (¾fl oz) lemon juice
15ml (½fl oz) sugar syrup (see page 21)
1 egg white
3 dashes of Angostura bitters, to
    garnish

In a cocktail shaker, dry shake all the
ingredients, then add ice cubes and
shake again. Fine-strain into a chilled
coupe and garnish with 3 dashes of
Angostura bitters.

Artifact Sour

MAKES 1 DRINK

25ml (1fl oz) Colombo London Dry Gin
15ml (½fl oz) Johnnie Walker Red
    Label Whisky
15ml (½fl oz) Lillet Blanc
20ml (¾fl oz) lemon juice
15ml (½fl oz) St Lawrence Gold Pure
    Maple Syrup
2 dashes of Bob's Chocolate Bitters
1 egg white
Raspberry powder, to garnish

In a cocktail shaker, dry shake all
the ingredients, then add ice cubes
and shake again. Fine-strain into
a chilled coupe and garnish with
raspberry powder.

✦ Credit: Ryan Chetiyawardana, Mr Lyan,
London

Continental Sour

MAKES 1 DRINK

40ml (1½fl oz) Rémy Martin VSOP
    Cognac
10ml (¼fl oz) Graham's Late Bottled
    Vintage Port
20ml (¾fl oz) lemon juice
10ml (¼fl oz) sugar syrup (see page 21)
1 egg white
Lemon coin, to garnish

In a cocktail shaker, dry shake all the
ingredients, then add ice cubes and
shake again. Fine-strain into a chilled
rocks glass over an ice block. Express
the lemon coin over the top, then
discard.

Pisco Sour

(frozen version)

MAKES 1 DRINK

50ml (2fl oz) Barsol Pisco
25ml (1fl oz) sugar syrup (see page 21)
10ml (¼fl oz) lime juice
10ml (¼fl oz) lemon juice
1 egg white
3 drops of Angostura bitters, to
    garnish

Blend all the ingredients with half
a scoop of crushed ice until silky
smooth. Pour into a chilled large
rocks glass and garnish with 3 drops
of Angostura bitters.

Pisco Sour

(shaken version)

MAKES 1 DRINK

50ml (2fl oz) Barsol Pisco
25ml (1fl oz) sugar syrup (see page 21)
10ml (¼fl oz) lime juice
10ml (¼fl oz) lemon juice
1 egg white
3 drops of Angostura bitters, to
    garnish

In a cocktail shaker, dry shake all
the ingredients, then add ice cubes
and hard shake until the shaker is
very cold. Strain into a chilled
coupe and garnish with 3 drops
of Angostura bitters.

Grasshopper

MAKES 1 DRINK

25ml (1fl oz) Briottet Crème de Cacao
    Blanc
25ml (1fl oz) Briottet Liqueur de
    Menthe Verte
40ml (1½fl oz) double cream
Grated chocolate, to garnish

In a cocktail shaker, shake all the
ingredients with ice cubes, then
fine-strain into a chilled coupe.
Garnish with grated chocolate.

✦ Credit: Tujague's, New Orleans

Brandy Alexander

MAKES 1 DRINK

35ml (1fl oz) Rémy Martin VSOP
    Cognac
20ml (¾fl oz) Giffard Crème de Cacao
    (brown)
25ml (1fl oz) double cream
3 dashes of Bob's Chocolate Bitters
Grated nutmeg, to garnish

In a cocktail shaker, shake all the
ingredients with ice cubes, then
fine-strain into a chilled coupe.
Garnish with grated nutmeg.

→ Overleaf, left to right
    Cosmopolitan (see page 86)
    Pisco Sour, shaken (see above)
    Ivy Gimlet (see page 134)
    Artist's Special (see page 85)

Solstice

MAKES 1 DRINK

50ml (2fl oz) Absolut Elyx
20ml (¾fl oz) Grapefruit Sherbet (see
    page 211)
25ml (1fl oz) lemon juice
3 dashes of rose water
1 egg white
25ml (1fl oz) Three Cents Pink
    Grapefruit Soda, to top up
Grapefruit twist, to garnish

In a cocktail shaker, dry shake all the
ingredients, except the grapefruit
soda, then add ice cubes and shake
again. Fine-strain into a flute and top
up with the grapefruit soda. Garnish
with a grapefruit twist.

✦ Credit: Joe Schofield, Schofield's Bar,
Manchester

Amelia

MAKES 1 DRINK

30ml (1fl oz) Macchu Pisco
25ml (1fl oz) Purple Corn (Chicha)
    Syrup (see page 196)
20ml (¾fl oz) lime juice
10ml (¼fl oz) Avuá Amburana Cachaça
10ml (¼fl oz) Lustau East India Solera
    Sherry
5ml (1 tsp) Salers Gentian Apéritif
6 dashes of Hella Smoked Chilli
    Bitters
1 egg white
Fever-Tree Soda Water, to top up
6 sprays of Sombra Mezcal, to garnish

In a cocktail shaker, dry shake all
the ingredients, except the soda
water, then add ice cubes and shake
again. Fine-strain into a fizz glass or
highball and top up with the soda
water. Garnish with 6 sprays of the
mezcal using an atomizer.

✦ Credit: Cristian Rodriguez, NoMad Bar,
New York

Clover Club

MAKES 1 DRINK

50ml (2fl oz) Plymouth Gin
20ml (¾fl oz) lemon juice
20ml (¾fl oz) sugar syrup (see
    page 21)
1 egg white
4 raspberries

In a cocktail shaker, dry shake all the
ingredients, then add ice cubes and
shake again. Fine-strain into a chilled
coupe.

✦ Credit: Paul E Lowe, *Drinks, How to Mix,
How to Serve* (1927)

Claridge's Club

MAKES 1 DRINK

30ml (1fl oz) Plymouth Gin
35ml (1fl oz) Rhubarb Cordial #1 (see
    page 193)
5ml (1 tsp) sugar syrup (see page 21)
20ml (¾fl oz) lemon juice
3 drops of Citric Acid Solution (see
    page 210)
3 slices of rhubarb
1 egg white

In a cocktail shaker, dry shake all the
ingredients, then add ice cubes and
shake again. Fine-strain into a chilled
coupe.

✦ Credit: Alice Taraschi, The Fumoir,
London

Perfect Lady

MAKES 1 DRINK

40ml (1½fl oz) Plymouth Gin
10ml (¼fl oz) Briottet Crème d'Abricot
20ml (¾fl oz) lemon juice
10ml (¼fl oz) sugar syrup (see page 21)
1 egg white

In a cocktail shaker, dry shake all the ingredients, then add ice cubes and shake again. Fine-strain into a chilled coupe.

✦ Credit: Sidney Cox, Grosvenor House, London

Pink Lady

MAKES 1 DRINK

35ml (1fl oz) Plymouth Gin
15ml (½fl oz) Adrien Camut 6 Year Old Calvados
20ml (¾fl oz) lemon juice
15ml (½fl oz) sugar syrup (see page 21)
5ml (1 tsp) Bristol Syrup Company Grenadine
1 egg white

In a cocktail shaker, dry shake all the ingredients, then add ice cubes and shake again. Fine-strain into a chilled coupe.

✦ Credit: Jacques Straub, *Straub's Manual of Mixed Drinks* (1913)

White Russian

MAKES 6 DRINKS

305ml (10½fl oz) Milk-washed Coffee Vodka (see page 207)
275ml (9½fl oz) water
90ml (3fl oz) Miso Syrup (see page 194)

Mix all the ingredients in a large jug, then pour into a 750ml (25½fl oz) bottle and store in the refrigerator. To serve, pour 100ml (3½fl oz) of the cocktail into a chilled rocks glass over an ice block.

✦ Credit: Max Venning, Three Sheets, London

White Lady

MAKES 1 DRINK

45ml (1½fl oz) Plymouth Gin
15ml (½fl oz) Cointreau
20ml (¾fl oz) lemon juice
15ml (½fl oz) sugar syrup (see page 21)
1 egg white

In a cocktail shaker, dry shake all the ingredients, then add ice cubes and shake again. Fine-strain into a chilled coupe.

✦ Credit: Harry MacElhone, Harry's New York Bar, Paris

Rattlesnake

MAKES 1 DRINK

50ml (2fl oz) Michter's US*1 Kentucky Straight Rye Whiskey
20ml (¾fl oz) lemon juice
20ml (¾fl oz) sugar syrup (see page 21)
2 dashes of Pernod Absinthe
1 egg white

In a cocktail shaker, dry shake all the ingredients, then add ice cubes and shake again. Fine-strain into a chilled coupe.

✦ Credit: Harry Craddock, The Savoy, London

Champs-Élysées

40ml (1½fl oz) Rémy Martin VSOP
    Cognac
10ml (¼fl oz) Green Chartreuse
20ml (¾fl oz) lemon juice
10ml (¼fl oz) sugar syrup (see page 21)
1 dash of Angostura bitters
Lemon coin, to garnish

In a cocktail shaker, shake all the
ingredients with ice cubes, then fine-
strain into a chilled coupe. Express
the lemon coin over the top, then
discard.

✦ Credit: Nina Toye & A H Adair, *Drinks –
Long and Short* (1925)

Maid in Jalisco

MAKES 1 DRINK

40ml (1½fl oz) Tapatio Blanco Tequila
5ml (1 tsp) Belvoir Elderflower Cordial
15ml (½fl oz) agave syrup
20ml (¾fl oz) lime juice
4 cucumber slices, plus a cucumber
    coin, to garnish

In a cocktail shaker, shake all the
ingredients with ice cubes, then
fine-strain into a chilled rocks glass
over an ice block. Garnish with a
cucumber coin.

✦ Adapted by: Nathan McCarley-O'Neill,
Claridge's Bar, London

Apple Cider

MAKES 1 DRINK

30ml (1fl oz) Michter's US*1 Kentucky
    Straight Bourbon Whiskey
15ml (½fl oz) St George Spiced Pear
    Liqueur
150ml (5fl oz) Hot Spiced Cider (see
    page 215)
Grated nutmeg, to garnish

Fill a coffee glass with freshly boiled
water to warm. Pour the water away
and build the ingredients in the hot
glass. Garnish with grated nutmeg.
Serve hot.

Champs-Élysées #2020

MAKES 1 DRINK

40ml (1½fl oz) Martell Cordon Bleu
    Cognac
10ml (¼fl oz) Green Chartreuse
5ml (1 tsp) Ilegal Mezcal
20ml (¾fl oz) lemon juice
15ml (½fl oz) sugar syrup (see page 21)
2 dashes of Angostura bitters, plus a
    little extra, to garnish
4 mint leaves, plus an extra mint sprig,
    to garnish
Lemon twist, to garnish

In a cocktail shaker, shake all the
ingredients with ice cubes, then
fine-strain into a chilled punch
glass over crushed ice. Garnish with
6 additional dashes of bitters, the
lemon twist and a mint sprig.

✦ Adapted by: Denis Broci, Claridge's Bar,
London

Queen Street

MAKES 1 DRINK

50ml (2fl oz) Bacardí Carta Blanca
    Rum
20ml (¾fl oz) Martini Riserva Speciale
    Ambrato
20ml (¾fl oz) lemon juice
20ml (¾fl oz) sugar syrup (see
    page 21)
3 dashes of Bittered Sling Cascade
    Celery bitters
3 sprays of Laphroaig 10 Year Old
    Whisky, to garnish

In a cocktail shaker, shake all the
ingredients with ice cubes, then
fine-strain into a chilled coupe.
Garnish with 3 sprays of the
Laphroaig, using an atomizer.

✦ Credit: Panda & Sons, Edinburgh

→ Champs-Élysées #2020

Pastis Blanche

MAKES 1 DRINK

25ml (1fl oz) Pernod Absinthe
20ml (¾fl oz) still mineral water
20ml (¾fl oz) lemon juice
20ml (¾fl oz) Bristol Syrup Company
 Orgeat
10ml (¼fl oz) sugar syrup (see page 21)
6 dashes of Peychaud's bitters, to
 garnish
Mint sprig, to garnish

In a cocktail shaker, shake all the
ingredients with ice cubes, then
fine-strain into a chilled rocks glass
filled with crushed ice. Garnish with
6 dashes of Peychaud's bitters and
a mint sprig.

✦ Adapted by: Nathan McCarley-O'Neill,
The Painter's Room, London

Aviation

MAKES 1 DRINK

45ml (1½fl oz) Bombay Sapphire Gin
10ml (¼fl oz) Maraschino
5ml (1 tsp) Briottet Liqueur de Violette
20ml (¾fl oz) lemon juice
5ml (1 tsp) sugar syrup (see page 21)
Fabbri Amarena cherry, to garnish

In a cocktail shaker, shake all the
ingredients with ice cubes, then
fine-strain into a chilled coupe.
Garnish with the cherry.

✦ Credit: Hugo Ensslin, Hotel Wallick,
New York

Prescription Julep

MAKES 1 DRINK

30ml (1fl oz) Rémy Martin VSOP
 Cognac
30ml (1fl oz) Michter's US*1 Kentucky
 Straight Rye Whiskey
7.5ml (1½ tsp) Heather Honey Syrup
 (see page 194)
10 mint leaves, plus a mint sprig, to
 garnish

Churn all the ingredients in a julep tin
with crushed ice. Add more crushed
ice and churn until frozen, then cap
with a little more crushed ice (so it
looks like a snow cone). Garnish with
a mint sprig.

Charlie Chaplin

MAKES 1 DRINK

25ml (1fl oz) Plymouth Sloe Gin
25ml (1fl oz) Briottet Crème d'Abricot
25ml (1fl oz) lime juice
Lime wedge, to garnish

In a cocktail shaker, shake all the
ingredients with ice cubes, then
fine-strain into a chilled coupe.
Garnish with a lime wedge.

✦ Credit: Albert S Crockett, *The Old
Waldorf-Astoria Bar Book* (1934)

Mint Julep

MAKES 1 DRINK

65ml (2¼fl oz) Maker's Mark Bourbon
    Whisky
10ml (¼fl oz) sugar syrup (see page 21)
10 mint leaves, plus a mint sprig, to
    garnish

Churn all the ingredients in a chilled
julep tin with crushed ice. Add more
crushed ice and churn until frozen,
then cap with a little more crushed
ice (so it looks like a snow cone).
Garnish with a mint sprig.

Genus Apis

MAKES 1 DRINK

50ml (2fl oz) Maker's Mark Bourbon
    Whisky
25ml (1fl oz) Heather Honey Syrup
    (see page 194)
20ml (¾fl oz) pomegranate juice
20ml (¾fl oz) lemon juice
4 mint leaves, plus a mint sprig, to
    garnish
Pomegranate seeds, to garnish

Churn all the ingredients in a chilled
julep tin with crushed ice. Add
more crushed ice and churn until
frozen, then cap with a little more
crushed ice (so it looks like a snow
cone). Garnish with a mint sprig and
pomegranate seeds.

✦ Credit: Filippo Ricci, Claridge's Bar,
London

Conqueror

MAKES 1 DRINK

40ml (1½fl oz) Koch Espadín Mezcal
10ml (¼fl oz) Combier Triple Sec
10ml (¼fl oz) Briottet Crème de Cacao
    (Cocoa)
15ml (½fl oz) lemon juice
10ml (¼fl oz) Bristol Syrup Company
    Orgeat
5ml (1 tsp) sugar syrup (see page 21)
Grated nutmeg, to garnish

In a cocktail shaker, shake all the
ingredients with ice cubes, then
fine-strain into a chilled rocks glass
over an ice block. Garnish with grated
nutmeg.

✦ Adapted by: Nathan McCarley-O'Neill,
Claridge's Bar, London

Siesta

MAKES 1 DRINK

40ml (1½fl oz) Tapatio Blanco Tequila
10ml (¼fl oz) Campari
20ml (¾fl oz) grapefruit juice
10ml (¼fl oz) lime juice
15ml (½fl oz) sugar syrup (see page 21)

In a cocktail shaker, shake all
the ingredients with ice cubes.
Fine-strain into a chilled coupe.

✦ Credit: Katie Stripe, Flatiron Lounge,
New York

Picante

MAKES 1 DRINK

1 red jalapeño chilli, plus an extra chilli
    slice, to garnish
3 sprigs of coriander
50ml (2fl oz) Tapatio Blanco Tequila
20ml (¾fl oz) lime juice
15ml (½fl oz) agave syrup

Muddle the chilli and coriander
sprigs in a cocktail shaker, then add
the remaining ingredients and shake
with ice cubes. Fine-strain into a
chilled rocks glass over an ice block
and garnish with a slice of chilli.

✦ Credit: Chris Ojeda, Soho House
West Hollywood

Piquant

MAKES 1 DRINK

1 dash of Angostura bitters
15ml (½fl oz) Pierre Ferrand Dry
    Curaçao
15ml (½fl oz) Disaronno Amaretto
20ml (¾fl oz) Spicy Vanilla Honey (see
    page 198)
20ml (¾fl oz) lemon juice
40ml (1½fl oz) Belvedere Vodka
Bird's Eye chilli, sliced into rings, to
    garnish

In a cocktail shaker, shake all the
ingredients with ice cubes, then
fine-strain into a large chilled rocks
glass over an ice block. Garnish with
3 chilli rings.

Pinky Gonzalez

MAKES 1 DRINK

45ml (1½fl oz) Tapatio Blanco Tequila
15ml (½fl oz) Pierre Ferrand Dry
    Curaçao
20ml (¾fl oz) lemon juice
15ml (½fl oz) Bristol Syrup Company
    Orgeat
5ml (1 tsp) sugar syrup (see page 21)
1 dash of Angostura bitters
1 dash of Peychaud's bitters

TO GARNISH
Orange slice
Fabbri Amarena cherry
Mint sprig

In a cocktail shaker, short shake all
the ingredients with 3 ice cubes for
6–8 seconds, then fine-strain into
a chilled rocks glass over crushed
ice. Garnish with a slice of orange, a
cherry and a mint sprig.

Golden Cadillac

MAKES 1 DRINK

50ml (2fl oz) Tapatio Blanco Tequila
20ml (¾fl oz) lime juice
5ml (1 tsp) sugar syrup (see page 21)
15ml (½fl oz) Grand Marnier
Lime wedge, to garnish

In a cocktail shaker, shake all the
ingredients, except the Grand
Marnier, with ice cubes, then fine-
strain into a chilled rocks glass over
an ice block. Float the Grand Marnier
on top and garnish with a lime
wedge.

Toreador

MAKES 1 DRINK

40ml (1½fl oz) Ocho Blanco Tequila
15ml (½fl oz) Briottet Crème d'Abricot
15ml (½fl oz) lemon juice
10ml (¼fl oz) sugar syrup (see page 21)

In a cocktail shaker, shake all the
ingredients with ice cubes. Fine-
strain into a chilled coupe.

✦ Credit: William J Tarling, *Café Royal
Cocktail Book* (1937)

Last Stand

MAKES 1 DRINK

40ml (1½fl oz) Tapatio Blanco Tequila
15ml (½fl oz) Aperol
15ml (½fl oz) lemon juice
15ml (½fl oz) sugar syrup (see page 21)
10ml (¼fl oz) grapefruit juice
Orange wedge, to garnish

In a cocktail shaker, shake all the
ingredients with ice cubes, then
fine-strain into the glass over an
ice block. Garnish with an orange
wedge.

✦ Adapted by: Nathan McCarley-O'Neill,
Claridge's Bar, London

Wibble

25ml (1fl oz) Plymouth Gin
25ml (1fl oz) Plymouth Sloe Gin
5ml (1 tsp) Merlet Crème de Mûre
20ml (¾fl oz) grapefruit juice
5ml (1 tsp) lemon juice
10ml (¼fl oz) sugar syrup (see page 21)
Lemon twist, to garnish

In a cocktail shaker, shake all the ingredients with ice cubes, then fine-strain into a chilled coupe. Garnish with a lemon twist.

✦ Credit: Dick Bradsell, The Player, London

Margarita

MAKES 1 DRINK

Sea salt
50ml (2fl oz) Tapatio Blanco Tequila
15ml (½fl oz) Cointreau
15ml (½fl oz) lime juice
5ml (1 tsp) sugar syrup (see page 21)

Rim a chilled rocks glass with sea salt (see page 19). In a cocktail shaker, shake all the ingredients with ice cubes. Fine-strain into the glass over an ice block.

Mezcal Margarita

MAKES 1 DRINK

Sea salt
25ml (1fl oz) Tapatio Blanco Tequila
25ml (1fl oz) Ilegal Mezcal
15ml (½fl oz) Combier Triple Sec
20ml (¾fl oz) lime juice
5ml (1 tsp) sugar syrup (see page 21)
Lime wedge, to garnish

Rim a chilled rocks glass with sea salt (see page 19). In a cocktail shaker, shake all the ingredients with ice cubes. Fine-strain into the glass over an ice block and garnish with a lime wedge.

Tommy's Margarita

MAKES 1 DRINK

50ml (2fl oz) Ocho Blanco Tequila
20ml (¾fl oz) lime juice
20ml (¾fl oz) agave syrup
Lime wedge, to garnish

In a cocktail shaker, shake all the ingredients with ice cubes, then fine-strain into a chilled rocks glass over an ice block. Garnish with a lime wedge.

✦ Credit: Julio Bermejo, San Francisco

Pendennis

MAKES 1 DRINK

50ml (2fl oz) Plymouth Gin
20ml (¾fl oz) Briottet Crème d'Abricot
20ml (¾fl oz) lime juice
10ml (¼fl oz) sugar syrup (see page 21)
1 dash of Peychaud's bitters

In a cocktail shaker, shake all the ingredients with ice cubes. Fine-strain into a chilled coupe.

✦ Named after: Pendennis Club, Louisville, Kentucky

Cameron's Kick

MAKES 1 DRINK

25ml (1fl oz) Johnnie Walker Black Label Whisky
25ml (1fl oz) Powers John's Lane 12 Year Old Irish Whiskey
20ml (¾fl oz) lemon juice
15ml (½fl oz) Bristol Syrup Company Orgeat

In a cocktail shaker, shake all the ingredients with ice cubes. Fine-strain into a chilled coupe.

✦ Credit: Harry MacElhone, *ABC of Mixing Cocktails* (1923)

Ward Eight

MAKES 1 DRINK

50ml (2fl oz) Maker's Mark Bourbon
    Whisky
20ml (¾fl oz) lemon juice
15ml (½fl oz) sugar syrup (see page 21)
5ml (1 tsp) Bristol Syrup Company
    Grenadine
2 orange wedges

In a cocktail shaker, shake all the
ingredients with ice cubes. Fine-
strain into a chilled rocks glass over
an ice block.

✦ Credit: Robert Vermeire, *Cocktails: How
to Mix Them* (1922)

José Martí Especial

MAKES 1 DRINK

40ml (1½fl oz) Havana Club 3 Year
    Old Rum
15ml (½fl oz) Lustau Fino Sherry
20ml (¾fl oz) lime juice
15ml (½fl oz) sugar syrup (see page 21)
5ml (1 tsp) Pernod Absinthe
4 cloves

In a cocktail shaker, shake all
the ingredients with ice cubes.
Fine-strain into a chilled coupe.

✦ Credit: Andy Loudon, Satan's Whiskers,
London

Rhubarby

MAKES 1 DRINK

40ml (1½fl oz) Tanqueray No Ten
10ml (¼fl oz) Tarragon-infused Dolin
    Dry Vermouth (see page 207)
15ml (½fl oz) Rhubarb Syrup (see page
    196)
20ml (¾fl oz) Apple Citrus (see page
    214)
1 dash of orange bitters
1 dash of Pernod Absinthe
Grapefruit coin, to garnish

Stir all the ingredients in a mixing
glass with ice cubes, then strain
into a chilled coupe. Garnish with a
grapefruit coin.

✦ Credit: Nathan McCarley-O'Neill, Davies
and Brook, London

Somerset Sunset

MAKES 1 DRINK

30ml (1fl oz) Tanqueray London Dry
    Gin
30ml (1fl oz) Plymouth Sloe Gin
35ml (1fl oz) Eager Apple Juice
10ml (¼fl oz) lemon juice
5ml (1 tsp) sugar syrup (see page 21)
10 blueberries, plus 3 extra, to garnish

Muddle all the ingredients in a
cocktail shaker, then shake with
ice cubes. Fine-strain into a
chilled coupe and garnish with 3
blueberries skewered with a cocktail
stick on the rim.

✦ Credit: Wenek Bronk, Claridge's Bar,
London

Sidecar

MAKES 1 DRINK

Granulated sugar
50ml (2fl oz) Rémy Martin VSOP
    Cognac
20ml (¾fl oz) Cointreau
20ml (¾fl oz) lemon juice
10ml (¼fl oz) sugar syrup (see page 21)

Rim a chilled coupe with granulated sugar (see page 19). In a cocktail shaker, shake all the ingredients with ice cubes. Fine-strain into the glass.

✦ Credit: Harry MacElhone, *ABC of Mixing Cocktails* (1923)

Disco Ball

MAKES 1 DRINK

35ml (1fl oz) Sombra Mezcal
10ml (¼fl oz) Yellow Chartreuse
Fever-Tree Ginger Ale, to top up
Orange wedge, to garnish

Build the mezcal and chartreuse in a chilled rocks glass over an ice block. Top up with the ginger ale. Use a bar spoon to stir the ice gently, then garnish with an orange wedge.

✦ Credit: Matteo Carretta, Davies and Brook, London

Celery Fizz

MAKES 1 DRINK

2 sorrel leaves
30ml (1fl oz) Tapatio Blanco Tequila
7.5ml (1½ tsp) Svöl Danish-Style
    Aquavit
15ml (½fl oz) grapefruit juice
15ml (½fl oz) celery juice
15ml (½fl oz) lime juice
15ml (½fl oz) sugar syrup (see page 21)
1 egg white
5 dashes of Pernod Absinthe
4 dashes of Saline Solution (see
    page 210)
Fever-Tree Soda Water, to top up
Black pepper, to garnish

Place the sorrel leaves in a cocktail shaker, add the remaining ingredients, except the soda water, and dry shake. Add ice cubes, shake again, then fine-strain into a highball. Top up with the soda water and garnish with a pinch of black pepper.

✦ Credit: Pietro Collina, Davies and Brook, London

Maid in Cuba

MAKES 1 DRINK

50ml (2fl oz) Bacardí Carta Blanca
    Rum
20ml (¾fl oz) lime juice
12.5ml (2½ tsp) sugar syrup (see
    page 21)
3 dashes of Pernod Absinthe
5 mint leaves
2 cucumber slices, plus a cucumber
    coin, to garnish
Fever-Tree Soda Water, to top up

In a cocktail shaker, shake all the ingredients, except the soda water, with ice cubes, then fine-strain into a chilled coupe. Top up with the soda water and garnish with a cucumber coin.

✦ Credit: Tom Lasher-Walker, The Savoy, London

→ Celery Fizz

Mayahue

25ml (1fl oz) Ilegal Mezcal
25ml (1fl oz) Tapatio Blanco Tequila
15ml (½fl oz) Damiana Liqueur
20ml (¾fl oz) Pistachio Orgeat (see page 209)
25ml (1fl oz) lime juice
1 egg white
Chamomile buds, to garnish

In a cocktail shaker, dry shake all the ingredients, then add ice cubes and shake again. Strain into a chilled coupe and garnish with chamomile buds.

✦ **Credit: Gábor Onufer, The Fumoir, London**

The Maguey

MAKES 1 DRINK

40ml (1½fl oz) Koch Espadín Mezcal
10ml (¼fl oz) Bristol Syrup Company Coconut
7.5ml (1½ tsp) sugar syrup (see page 21)
20ml (¾fl oz) lemon juice
3 dashes of Pernod Absinthe
1 egg white
4 raspberries, plus 3 extra, to garnish

In a cocktail shaker, dry shake all the ingredients, then add ice cubes and shake again. Fine-strain into a chilled coupe and garnish with 3 raspberries skewered with a cocktail stick on the rim.

✦ **Credit: Luca Ponte, The Fumoir, London**

Pegu Club

MAKES 1 DRINK

45ml (1½fl oz) Plymouth Gin
15ml (½fl oz) Pierre Ferrand Dry Curaçao
20ml (¾fl oz) lime juice
10ml (¼fl oz) sugar syrup (see page 21)
1 dash of Angostura bitters
1 dash of orange bitters

In a cocktail shaker, shake all the ingredients with ice cubes. Fine-strain into a chilled coupe.

✦ **Credit: Pegu Club, British Colonial Rangoon, Burma (now Yangon, Myanmar)**

The Charles

MAKES 1 DRINK

Rind of 1 pink grapefruit
2ml (½ tsp) sugar syrup (see page 21)
60ml (2fl oz) Tanqueray No Ten
7.5ml (1½ tsp) La Feé Bohemian Absinthe
5ml (1 tsp) Luxardo Maraschino Liqueur
Fabbri Amarena cherry, to garnish

Muddle the grapefruit rind and sugar syrup in a mixing glass, then add the remaining ingredients and stir with ice cubes. Fine-strain into a chilled coupe and garnish with the cherry.

✦ **Credit: Brian Silva, Connaught Bar, Connaught Hotel, London**

Naked & Famous

MAKES 1 DRINK

20ml (¾fl oz) Del Maguey Chichicapa Mezcal
20ml (¾fl oz) Yellow Chartreuse
20ml (¾fl oz) Aperol
20ml (¾fl oz) lime juice

In a cocktail shaker, shake all the ingredients with ice cubes. Fine-strain into a chilled coupe.

✦ **Credit: Joaquín Simó, Death & Co, New York**

→ Mayahue

Goodfellas

MAKES 1 DRINK

40ml (1½fl oz) Cardamom-infused
  Maker's Mark Bourbon Whisky
  (see page 202)
20ml (¾fl oz) Cocchi Storico
  Vermouth Di Torino
10ml (¼fl oz) Black Cardamom Syrup
  (see page 197)
1 bar spoon balsamic vinegar
2 dashes of Bitter Truth Aromatic
  Bitters
Fabbri Amarena cherry, to garnish

In a cocktail shaker, shake all the
ingredients with ice cubes, then
fine-strain into a chilled wine glass
with ice cubes. Garnish with the
cherry.

✦ Credit: Giorgio Bargiani, Connaught Bar,
London

Walcott Express

MAKES 1 DRINK

45ml (1½fl oz) Emile Pernot Grande
  Liqueur de Sapins
15ml (½fl oz) Germain-Robin VSOP
  Cognac
5ml (1 tsp) Giffard Crème de Menthe
20ml (¾fl oz) lime juice
20ml (¾fl oz) Rose's Lime Juice
  Cordial
4 mint leaves

In a cocktail shaker, shake all
the ingredients with ice cubes.
Fine-strain into a chilled coupe.

✦ Credit: Will Elliot, Maison Premiere,
New York

Robin Hood, Quince of Thieves

MAKES 1 DRINK

40ml (1½fl oz) Somerset 5 Year Old
  Cider Brandy
20ml (¾fl oz) Bramley & Gage Quince
  Liqueur
20ml (¾fl oz) lemon juice
15ml (½fl oz) thyme honey
Brover Mini Apple in Syrup, to garnish

In a cocktail shaker, shake all the
ingredients with ice cubes, then
fine-strain into a chilled coupe.
Garnish with a mini apple on a
cocktail stick.

✦ Credit: Gareth Evans, The Blind Pig,
London

Pan American Clipper

MAKES 1 DRINK

40ml (1½fl oz) Adrien Camut 6 Year
  Old Calvados
20ml (¾fl oz) lime juice
12.5ml (2½ tsp) Bristol Syrup
  Company Grenadine
5ml (1 tsp) sugar syrup (see page 21)
2 dashes of Pernod Absinthe

In a cocktail shaker, shake all
the ingredients with ice cubes.
Fine-strain into a chilled coupe.

✦ Credit: Charles H Baker Jr,
The Gentleman's Companion (1939)

The Landmark of Mayfair

MAKES 1 DRINK

45ml (1½fl oz) Beefeater London Dry
  Gin
10ml (¼fl oz) Green Chartreuse
10ml (¼fl oz) Wolfschmidt Kummel
20ml (¾fl oz) lemon juice
10ml (¼fl oz) sugar syrup (see page 21)
Fabbri Amarena cherry, to garnish

In a cocktail shaker, shake all the
ingredients with ice cubes, then
fine-strain into a chilled coupe.
Garnish with the cherry.

✦ Adapted by: Nathan McCarley-O'Neill,
Claridge's Bar, London

Bardot

MAKES 1 DRINK

35ml (1fl oz) Belvedere Vodka
15ml (½fl oz) Lustau Fino Sherry
5ml (1 tsp) Merlet Crème de Cassis
15ml (½fl oz) sugar syrup (see page 21)
20ml (¾fl oz) lemon juice
2 dashes of Bob's Orange & Mandarin
    Bitters
Mandarin coin, to garnish

In a cocktail shaker, shake all the ingredients with ice cubes, then fine-strain into a chilled coupe over an ice block. Express the mandarin coin over the top, then discard.

✦ **Credit: Nathan McCarley-O'Neill, The Fumoir, London**

Gin Basil Smash

MAKES 1 DRINK

50ml (2fl oz) Plymouth Gin
20ml (¾fl oz) sugar syrup (see
    page 21)
3 lemon wedges, plus an extra wedge,
    to garnish
8 basil leaves

In a cocktail shaker, shake all the ingredients with ice cubes, then fine-strain into a chilled rocks glass over an ice block. Garnish with a lemon wedge.

✦ **Credit: Joerg Meyer, Le Lion – Bar De Paris, Hamburg**

Apple Jack Rabbit

MAKES 1 DRINK

50ml (2fl oz) Adrien Camut 6 Year Old
    Calvados
15ml (½fl oz) St Lawrence Gold Pure
    Maple Syrup
15ml (½fl oz) orange juice
15ml (½fl oz) lemon juice
Orange slice, to garnish

In a cocktail shaker, shake all the ingredients with ice cubes, then fine-strain into a chilled rocks glass over an ice block. Garnish with a slice of orange.

✦ **Credit: Harry Craddock, The Savoy, London**

Whisky Smash

MAKES 1 DRINK

50ml (2fl oz) Maker's Mark Bourbon
    Whisky
20ml (¾fl oz) sugar syrup (see
    page 21)
8 mint leaves, plus a mint sprig, to
    garnish
3 lemon wedges, plus an extra wedge,
    to garnish

Muddle all the ingredients in a cocktail shaker, then shake with ice cubes. Fine-strain into a chilled rocks glass filled with crushed ice. Garnish with a mint sprig and a lemon wedge.

✦ **Credit: Dale DeGroff, The Rainbow Room, New York**

Bee's Knees

MAKES 1 DRINK

50ml (2fl oz) Plymouth Gin
20ml (¾fl oz) Heather Honey Syrup
    (see page 194)
20ml (¾fl oz) lemon juice

In a cocktail shaker, shake all the ingredients with ice cubes. Fine-strain into a chilled coupe.

Brigadoon

MAKES 1 DRINK

50ml (2fl oz) Johnnie Walker Black
    Label Whisky
20ml (¾fl oz) Briottet Crème
    d'Abricot
20ml (¾fl oz) lemon juice
5ml (1 tsp) Bristol Syrup Company
    Orgeat

In a cocktail shaker, shake all the ingredients with ice cubes. Fine-strain into a chilled coupe.

✦ **Credit: Adam McGurk, The Player, London**

Blinker

MAKES 1 DRINK

6 sprays of Pernod Absinthe, plus a
little extra, to rinse
45ml (1½fl oz) Michter's US*1
Kentucky Straight Rye Whiskey
35ml (1fl oz) grapefruit juice
10ml (¼fl oz) lemon juice
7.5ml (1½ tsp) Bristol Syrup Company
Grenadine

Spritz the inside of a cocktail shaker
with 6 light sprays of absinthe, using
an atomizer. Shake all the ingredients
with ice cubes, then fine-strain into
a chilled coupe that has been rinsed
with a little absinthe.

✦ Credit: Gavin Duffy, *The Official Mixer's
Manual* (1934)

Kentucky Maid

MAKES 1 DRINK

50ml (2fl oz) Michter's US*1 Kentucky
Straight Bourbon Whiskey
20ml (¾fl oz) lime juice
20ml (¾fl oz) sugar syrup (see
page 21)
5 mint leaves
Slice of cucumber, plus a cucumber
coin, to garnish

In a cocktail shaker, shake all the
ingredients with ice cubes, then
fine-strain into a chilled rocks glass
over an ice block. Garnish with a
cucumber coin.

✦ Credit: Sam Ross, Milk & Honey,
New York

Green Beast

MAKES 1 DRINK

2 cucumber slices, plus a cucumber
coin, to garnish
25ml (1fl oz) Pernod Absinthe
20ml (¾fl oz) still mineral water
20ml (¾fl oz) lime juice
15ml (½fl oz) sugar syrup (see page 21)

Muddle the cucumber slices in
a cocktail shaker, then add the
remaining ingredients and shake
with ice cubes. Fine-strain into a
chilled rocks glass over an ice block
and garnish with a cucumber coin.

✦ Credit: Charles Vexenat, Paris

The Duchess

MAKES 1 DRINK

50ml (2fl oz) Bacardí Ron Superior
Heritage Limited Edition
35ml (1fl oz) Pomelo Shrub (see
page 191)
10ml (¼fl oz) Italicus Rosolio Di
Bergamotto
5ml (1 tsp) Heather Honey Syrup (see
page 194)
20ml (¾fl oz) lime juice
3 dashes of Smoked Saline Solution
(see page 211)

In a cocktail shaker, shake all
the ingredients with ice cubes.
Fine-strain into a chilled coupe.

Silver Beet

MAKES 1 DRINK

30ml (1fl oz) Roku Gin
20ml (¾fl oz) Barsol Pisco
25ml (1fl oz) Roasted Beet Syrup (see
page 197)
20ml (¾fl oz) lime juice
1 egg white
Grated nutmeg, to garnish

In a cocktail shaker, dry shake all the
ingredients, then add ice cubes and
shake again. Fine-strain into a chilled
coupe over and ice block and garnish
with grated nutmeg.

✦ Credit: Gianluca Grimaldi, Claridge's Bar,
London

Italian Greyhound

MAKES 1 DRINK

Sea salt
30ml (1fl oz) Plymouth Gin
10ml (¼fl oz) Campari
40ml (1½fl oz) grapefruit juice
15ml (½fl oz) lemon juice
20ml (¾fl oz) sugar syrup (see
page 21)
Orange slice, to garnish

Rim a chilled rocks glass with sea salt
(see page 19). In a cocktail shaker,
shake all the ingredients with ice
cubes, then fine-strain into the rocks
glass over an ice block. Garnish with
a slice of orange.

Call Me Denzel

MAKES 1 DRINK

40ml (1½fl oz) Ron Zacapa 23
    Centenario
10ml (¼fl oz) Amaro Montenegro
15ml (½fl oz) lime juice
10ml (¼fl oz) sugar syrup (see page 21)
2 dashes of liquorice bitters
1 dash of Bob's Chocolate Bitters
Orange coin, to garnish

In a cocktail shaker, shake all the
ingredients with ice cubes, then fine-
strain into a chilled coupe. Garnish
with an orange coin.

✦ **Credit: Denis Broci, Claridge's Bar,
London**

Infante

MAKES 1 DRINK

50ml (2fl oz) Tapatio Blanco Tequila
20ml (¾fl oz) lime juice
15ml (½fl oz) Bristol Syrup Company
    Orgeat
1 dash of orange flower water
Lime wedge, to garnish
Grated nutmeg, to garnish

In a cocktail shaker, shake all the
ingredients with ice cubes, then
fine-strain into a chilled rocks glass
over an ice block. Garnish with a lime
wedge and a little grated nutmeg.

✦ **Credit: Giuseppe González, Suffolk Arms,
New York**

Irish Maid

MAKES 1 DRINK

50ml (2fl oz) Redbreast 12 Year Old
    Whiskey
5ml (1 tsp) St-Germain elderflower
    liqueur
20ml (¾fl oz) lemon juice
15ml (½fl oz) sugar syrup (see page 21)
2 cucumber slices, plus a cucumber
    coin, to garnish

In a cocktail shaker, shake all the
ingredients with ice cubes, then
fine-strain into a chilled rocks glass
over an ice block. Garnish with a
cucumber coin.

✦ **Credit: Jack McGarry, The Dead Rabbit,
New York**

Brown Derby

MAKES 1 DRINK

40ml (1½fl oz) Maker's Mark Bourbon
    Whisky
30ml (1fl oz) grapefruit juice
10ml (¼fl oz) lime juice
10ml (¼fl oz) Heather Honey Syrup
    (see page 194)

In a cocktail shaker, shake all the
ingredients with ice cubes. Fine-
strain into a chilled coupe.

Casino

MAKES 1 DRINK

50ml (2fl oz) Plymouth Gin
15ml (½fl oz) Maraschino
20ml (¾fl oz) lemon juice
5ml (1 tsp) sugar syrup (see page 21)
2 dashes of orange bitters
Orange coin, to garnish

In a cocktail shaker, shake all the
ingredients with ice cubes, then fine-
strain into a chilled coupe. Express
the orange coin over the top, then
discard.

✦ **Credit: Hugo R Ensslin, *Recipes for Mixed
Drinks* (1916 & 1917)**

Lumière

MAKES 1 DRINK

25ml (1fl oz) Ricard Pastis de Marseille
20ml (¾fl oz) still mineral water
15ml (½fl oz) sugar syrup (see page 21)
20ml (¾fl oz) lemon juice
4 mint leaves, plus a mint sprig, to
    garnish
2 cucumber slices

In a cocktail shaker, shake all the
ingredients with ice cubes, then fine-
strain into a chilled absinthe glass.
Garnish with a mint sprig.

✦ **Adapted by: Nathan McCarley-O'Neill,
The Fumoir, London**

Brandy Crusta

MAKES 1 DRINK

Caster sugar
50ml (2fl oz) Pierre Ferrand 1840
 Original Formula Cognac
7.5ml (1½ tsp) Cointreau
7.5ml (1½ tsp) Maraschino
15ml (½fl oz) lemon juice
15ml (½fl oz) sugar syrup (see page 21)
2 dashes of Angostura bitters
Lemon horse's neck, to garnish

Rim a chilled crusta glass with caster
sugar (see page 19). In a cocktail
shaker, shake all the ingredients with
ice cubes. Fine-strain into the glass
and garnish with a lemon horse's
neck.

✦ Credit: Joseph Santini, New Orleans

Bee Pollen Crusta

MAKES 1 DRINK

Bee pollen powder
45ml (1½fl oz) Konik's Tail Vodka
15ml (½fl oz) Rooibos-infused Noilly
 Prat Original Dry Vermouth (see
 page 207)
25ml (1fl oz) mandarin juice
15ml (½fl oz) lemon juice
10ml (¼fl oz) Chestnut Honey Syrup
 (see page 194)

Rim the outside of a chilled coupe
with bee pollen powder (see page
19), so that the glass is fully coated.
In a cocktail shaker, shake all the
ingredients with ice cubes, then
fine-strain into the glass.

✦ Credit: Vincenzo Pagliara, The Fumoir,

Cubanada

MAKES 1 DRINK

50ml (2fl oz) Havana Club 7 Year Old
 Rum
20ml (¾fl oz) lime juice
15ml (½fl oz) St Lawrence Gold Pure
 Maple Syrup
Lime twist, to garnish

In a cocktail shaker, shake all the
ingredients with ice cubes, then
fine-strain into a chilled coupe.
Garnish with a lime twist.

Apple Car

MAKES 1 DRINK

Caster sugar
50ml (2fl oz) Adrien Camut 6 Year Old
 Calvados
20ml (¾fl oz) Combier Triple Sec
20ml (¾fl oz) lemon juice

Rim a chilled coupe with caster sugar
(see page 19). In a cocktail shaker,
shake all the ingredients with ice
cubes, then fine-strain into the glass.

Ivy Gimlet

MAKES 1 DRINK

50ml (2fl oz) Ketel One Vodka
20ml (¾fl oz) lime juice
20ml (¾fl oz) sugar syrup (see
 page 21)
4 mint leaves

In a cocktail shaker, shake all
the ingredients with ice cubes.
Fine-strain into a chilled coupe.

→ Bee Pollen Crusta

The punchbowl

Punch is perhaps the original cocktail. It is also one of the most maligned – and has been subject to gross misinterpretations over the years. Much like a great party guestlist, it can contain disparate elements, surprises and bold ingredients, but needs to be treated with care and attention. There are recipes dating back to the 17th century for this concoction of spirit, citrus, sugar, spice and water, primarily drunk by British sailors aboard ships far from the taverns and ale of England. A silver punch-bowl was the accessory du jour for much of the 1700s, as punch was imbibed in coffee houses and drawing rooms in great quantities across London.

Although punch fell out of fashion during the Victorian era, it has seen a revival in recent years. At Claridge's, after much research and experimentation using historical recipes, punch has become something of a fixture on the menus. Served in the right glassware, in the correct environment, punch can be at once both refined and refreshing.

When legendary New York bar The Dead Rabbit popped up at Claridge's in the summer of 2017, transforming Claridge's Bar into a 'mid-19th-century Irish drinking tavern' for a week, a welcome punch was essential: Dead Rabbit is known for its revival of punches. Guests entered the bar with sawdust rustling underfoot to the sound of ragtime piano, and were greeted by a large china punchbowl, from which teacups of Bunny Boiler punch were ladled (see page 138).

To create a cocktail as elegant as a chequerboard foyer, Claridge's needed something a little smoother and more refined than the traditional brash flavours associated with punch. Hence the clarified milk punch – a punch that has had milk added to it, causing the citrus and milk to curdle, and then is strained through a coffee filter. The milk proteins act as a net, catching much of the colour pigment as well as some of the sugar. The resultant drink is marvellously translucent, with all the taste of the original ingredients in a more mellow formulation.

Such gastronomic chemistry is not new: milk punches have been around since the 18th century, when milk was often added to punch as a way of counteracting the acidity and harshness of the citrus and spirit. Today, Claridge's pays homage to the past with contemporary, seasonal flavours. At Davies and Brook, the flavour of the punch changes with the seasons: green apple and nori in spring, strawberry and coconut in summer, pear and bergamot in autumn and pineapple in winter. The clarification process means that each of these drinks looks very similar: that is, not unlike water. But the taste of each is dramatically different.

Strawberry & Coconut Punch

60ml (2fl oz) Plymouth Gin
35ml (1fl oz) Cocchi Rosa
25ml (1fl oz) Cocchi Americano
50ml (2fl oz) Chamomile Tea Cold
    Brew (see page 212)
30ml (1fl oz) lemon juice
30ml (1fl oz) milk
15ml (½fl oz) Bristol Syrup Company
    Coconut
5ml (1 tsp) sugar syrup (see page 21)
3 dashes of SélectArôme strawberry
    flavouring

Mix all the ingredients in a mixing glass, then rest for 10 minutes. Once it starts curdling, strain through a paper coffee filter (make sure you rinse the coffee filter before using). Serve immediately in a chilled rocks glass or keep in the refrigerator for up to 4 weeks if you are making a larger quantity to serve friends.

✦ **Credit: Matteo Carretta, Davies and Brook, London**

Pear & Bergamot Punch

MAKES 1 DRINK

60ml (2fl oz) Plymouth Gin
40ml (1½fl oz) Italicus Rosolio Di
    Bergamotto
25ml (1fl oz) Noilly Prat Original Dry
    Vermouth
25ml (1fl oz) Cocchi Americano
50ml (2fl oz) Bergamot Tea Cold Brew
    (see page 212)
30ml (1fl oz) lemon juice
30ml (1fl oz) milk
20ml (¾fl oz) Bristol Syrup Company
    Vanilla
5 dashes of SélectArôme pear
    flavouring

Mix all the ingredients in a mixing glass, then rest for 10 minutes.

Once it starts curdling, strain through a paper coffee filter (make sure you rinse the coffee filter before using). Serve immediately in a chilled rocks glass or keep in the refrigerator for up to 4 weeks if you are making a larger quantity to serve to friends.

✦ **Credit: Matteo Carretta, Davies and Brook, London**

Float Like A Butterfly

750g (1lb 10oz) fresh pineapple,
    chopped, including skin
250g (9oz) caster sugar
20g (¾oz) fennel seeds
100g (3½oz) lemon rind
200g (7oz) celery, chopped
300ml (10fl oz) lemon verbena tea
350ml (12fl oz) Maker's Mark Bourbon
    Whisky
200ml (7fl oz) Tapatio Blanco Tequila
75ml (2½fl oz) Pernod Absinthe
160ml (5½fl oz) lemon juice
300ml (10fl oz) milk

Put the pineapple, sugar, fennel
seeds, lemon rind and celery into
a large container and muddle well.
Add the lemon verbena tea, the
spirits and 100ml (3½fl oz) of the
lemon juice and leave to rest for
24 hours. Fine-strain into another
large container and seal with a lid.

Heat the milk without letting it boil.
Slowly pour the hot milk and the
remaining lemon juice into the
container of punch and leave to
infuse for 30 minutes.

Strain the punch through 2 muslin
cloths and leave to rest for 5 hours.

Strain again into a bottle and keep
in the refrigerator for up to 4 weeks.
To serve, stir the punch in a mixing
glass, then strain into flutes.

✦ **Credit: Maura Milia, Connaught Bar,
London**

Bunny Boiler

MAKES 6 DRINKS

360ml (12½fl oz) Manuka Tea-infused
    Banks 5 Island Rum (see page
    204)
125ml (4fl oz) lemon juice
125ml (4fl oz) Lemon Sherbet (see
    page 211)
45ml (1½fl oz) John D Taylor's Velvet
    Falernum
Lemon and pink grapefruit slices, to
    garnish

In a cocktail shaker, shake all the
ingredients with ice cubes, then pour
into a punchbowl over a large block
of ice. Garnish with slices of lemon
and pink grapefruit. To serve, strain
into teacups.

✦ **Credit: Jillian Vose, The Dead Rabbit,
New York**

Osaka Punch

MAKES 1 DRINK

40ml (1½fl oz) Roku Gin
15ml (½fl oz) Briottet Crème de Pêche
40ml (1½fl oz) cold Oolong Tea (see
    page 210)
15ml (½fl oz) lemon juice
5ml (1 tsp) sugar syrup (see page 21)
Grated nutmeg, to garnish

In a cocktail shaker, short shake all
the ingredients with 3 ice cubes for
6–8 seconds, then fine-strain into a
chilled rock glass over an ice block.
Garnish with grated nutmeg.

✦ **Credit: George Raju, The Fumoir, London**

→ Osaka Punch

Long
&
Refreshing

Just the tonic

Given the prowess of the bartenders at the hotel, it might seem baffling to even call a G&T a 'cocktail'. However, at Claridge's, a good G&T – preferably made with one part high-quality gin to four parts cold, effervescent tonic, served in a chilled highball packed tightly with ice cubes to the very top – is considered to be one of the finest of drinks. It is instantly refreshing, quintessentially British and the perfect 6pm livener.

It is also one of the very ripest for experimentation. Try your chosen gin with different tonics. Fever-Tree has a subtler bubble than the more boldly carbonated Schweppes: each will bring something different to the drink. The very adventurous might even consider a flavoured tonic. Today, there is a huge range, many all-natural and without artificial sweeteners (London Essence Co.'s Pomelo and Pink Pepper is a particular favourite).

Research different garnishes: the same gin will taste quite different with a slice of pink grapefruit expressed over the top. A London Dry gin such as Beefeater is juniper and citrus-forward, meaning a lemon slice works well; with Tanqueray No Ten, a lime or grapefruit wedge brings out those botanicals and adds an extra dimension to the drink. Hendrick's, meanwhile, is distilled with cucumber and rose, so a slice of cucumber will bring out the aromatics beautifully. The key is to experiment – try adding a slice of green apple, some mint or a raspberry or two. And why not a dash of Angostura bitters to finish?

Indeed, gin isn't even a prerequisite. Every country has its own classic combination of spirit, mixer and garnish, from a Portuguese white port, tonic and orange slice to a Mexican tequila, soda and lime (here, try using Three Cents Pink Grapefruit Soda) or the Argentinian hangover cure of Fernet-Branca and Coca-Cola.

THE PERFECT SERVE

Fill a chilled glass all the way to the top with ice cubes. Pour 50ml (2fl oz) of your chosen spirit over the ice, then add the mixer by pouring it slowly down the inside of the glass – not from a great height – trying to minimize contact with the ice. This will keep the mixer as carbonated as possible and minimize dilution.

Now carefully insert a bar spoon to the bottom of the glass, trying not to unduly disturb the ice, and turn the ingredients and ice one full rotation. Pivot the spoon directly under the bottom ice cube, lift the ice 2–3cm (¾–1¼in) from the bottom of the glass and shake the spoon lightly – a raft of bubbles will shoot up – then slowly drop the ice back and remove the spoon from the glass. Your drink has now been suitably woken up. As with every aspect of the hotel, it is the small details that make the biggest difference.

Tom Collins

MAKES 1 DRINK

50ml (2fl oz) Plymouth Gin
15ml (½fl oz) lemon juice
15ml (½fl oz) sugar syrup (see page 21)
2 bar spoons caster sugar
1 lemon wedge, plus an extra lemon
    wedge, to garnish
Fever-Tree Soda Water, to top up
Fabbri Amarena cherry, to garnish

In a cocktail shaker, shake all the
ingredients, except the soda water,
with ice cubes. Strain into a chilled
highball filled with ice cubes. Top up
with the soda water and garnish with
a lemon wedge and the cherry.

✦ Credit: Limmer's Hotel, London

Gin Rickey

MAKES 1 DRINK

50ml (2fl oz) Tanqueray London Dry
    Gin
15ml (½fl oz) sugar syrup (see page 21)
15ml (½fl oz) lime juice
2 bar spoons caster sugar
Fever-Tree Soda Water, to top up
Lime wedge, to garnish

In a cocktail shaker, shake all the
ingredients, except the soda water,
with ice cubes. Strain into a chilled
highball filled with ice cubes. Top up
with the soda water and garnish with
a lime wedge.

Gin & Tonic

MAKES 1 DRINK

50ml (2fl oz) Plymouth Gin
125ml (4fl oz) Fever-Tree Premium
    Indian Tonic Water
Lime wedge, to garnish

Build the gin and tonic water in a
chilled highball filled with ice cubes.
Garnish with a lime wedge.

G&T Alfresco

MAKES 1 DRINK

50ml (2fl oz) Plymouth Gin
10ml (¼fl oz) Cynar Amaro
2 drops of orange bitters
125ml (4fl oz) Fever-Tree Premium
    Indian Tonic Water
Cucumber slice, to garnish
Orange slice, to garnish

Build the ingredients in a chilled
highball filled with ice cubes. Garnish
with a cucumber slice and a slice of
orange.

Hayes Fizz

MAKES 1 DRINK

40ml (1½fl oz) Plymouth Gin
20ml (¾fl oz) lemon juice
20ml (¾fl oz) sugar syrup (see
    page 21)
2 dashes of Pernod Absinthe
Fever-Tree Soda Water, to top up

In a cocktail shaker, shake all the
ingredients, except the soda water,
with ice cubes. Strain into a chilled
highball filled with ice cubes and top
up with the soda water.

→ Tom Collins

Maison Absinthe Colada

MAKES 1 DRINK

20ml (¾fl oz) Pernod Absinthe
20ml (¾fl oz) Clément Rhum Blanc
　　Agricole
10ml (¼fl oz) Giffard Crème de
　　Menthe
50ml (2fl oz) pineapple juice
15ml (½fl oz) coconut cream
Mint sprig, to garnish

In a cocktail shaker, shake all the
ingredients with ice cubes, then
strain into a chilled highball filled
with crushed ice. Garnish with a
mint sprig.

✦ Credit: Natasha David and Maxwell
Britten, Maison Premiere, New York

Hurricane

MAKES 1 DRINK

30ml (1fl oz) Gosling's Black Seal Rum
30ml (1fl oz) Bacardí Ron Superior
　　Heritage Limited Edition
35ml (1fl oz) pineapple juice
35ml (1fl oz) orange juice
25ml (1fl oz) lime juice
15ml (½fl oz) passionfruit syrup
15ml (½fl oz) sugar syrup (see page 21)
2 dashes of Angostura bitters
Orange slice, to garnish

In a cocktail shaker, short shake all
the ingredients with 3 ice cubes for
6–8 seconds, then fine-strain into a
chilled punch glass over crushed ice.
Garnish with a slice of orange.

✦ Credit: Pat O'Brien's, New Orleans

Eastham & Carrie

MAKES 1 DRINK

60ml (2fl oz) Rum Blend Batch (see
　　page 206)
30ml (1fl oz) lime juice
25ml (1fl oz) Bristol Syrup Company
　　Orgeat
5ml (1 tsp) Wray & Nephew White
　　Overproof Rum

TO GARNISH
Mint sprig
Fabbri Amarena cherry
Lime wedge
Orange wedge

In a cocktail shaker, shake all the
ingredients with ice cubes, then
fine-strain into a chilled highball
over crushed ice. Garnish with a
mint sprig, a cherry, and lime
and orange wedges.

✦ Credit: Nathan McCarley-O'Neill,
The Painter's Room, London

Madison Avenue

MAKES 1 DRINK

45ml (1½fl oz) Bacardí Carta Blanca
　　Rum
20ml (¾fl oz) Combier Triple Sec
20ml (¾fl oz) lime juice
15ml (½fl oz) sugar syrup (see page 21)
2 dashes of orange bitters
5 mint leaves, plus a mint sprig, to
　　garnish

In a cocktail shaker, shake all the
ingredients, then fine-strain into a
chilled rocks glass filled with crushed
ice. Garnish with a mint sprig.

✦ Credit: Eddie Woelke, New York

Chicago Fizz

MAKES 1 DRINK

35ml (1fl oz) Bacardí 8 Year Old Rum
20ml (¾fl oz) Graham's Late Bottled
　　Vintage Port
20ml (¾fl oz) lemon juice
15ml (½fl oz) sugar syrup (see page 21)
1 egg white
Fever-Tree Soda Water, to top up

In a cocktail shaker, dry shake all
the ingredients, except the soda
water. Add ice cubes and shake
again. Strain into a chilled highball
over ice cubes and top up with the
soda water.

➔ Maison Absinthe Colada

Vodka & Soda

MAKES 1 DRINK

50ml (2fl oz) Belvedere Vodka
Fever-Tree Premium Soda Water, to
    top up
Lime wedge, to garnish

Build the vodka in a chilled highball over ice cubes, then top up with the soda water. Use a bar spoon to stir gently. Garnish with a lime wedge.

Salty Dog

MAKES 1 DRINK

Sea salt
50ml (2fl oz) Ketel One Vodka
100ml (3½fl oz) grapefruit juice
10ml (¼fl oz) sugar syrup (see page 21)

Half-rim a chilled highball with sea salt (see page 19). Build the ingredients in the glass over ice cubes.

Apple Collins

MAKES 1 DRINK

40ml (1½fl oz) Horseradish-infused
    Plymouth Gin (see page 204)
15ml (½fl oz) Heather Honey Syrup
    (see page 194)
15ml (½fl oz) apple juice
7.5ml (1½ tsp) Cinnamon Bark Syrup
    (see page 195)
6 dashes of Citric Acid Solution (see
    page 210)
2 dashes of Pernod Absinthe
Ground cinnamon, to garnish

In a cocktail shaker, shake all the ingredients with ice cubes, then fine-strain into a chilled juice glass over an ice block. Garnish with ground cinnamon.

✦ Credit: Nathan McCarley-O'Neill, Davies and Brook, London

Floradora

MAKES 1 DRINK

40ml (1½fl oz) Plymouth Gin
15ml (½fl oz) lime juice
10ml (¼fl oz) Ginger Syrup (see
    page 195)
10ml (¼fl oz) sugar syrup (see page 21)
2 raspberries, plus an extra raspberry,
    to garnish
Fever-Tree Ginger Ale, to top up
Lime wedge, to garnish

In a cocktail shaker, shake all the ingredients, except the ginger ale, with ice cubes, then strain into a chilled highball filled with ice cubes. Top up with the ginger ale and garnish with a raspberry and a lime wedge.

✦ Credit: J A Grohusko, *Jack's Manual* (1908)

Cucumber Collins

MAKES 1 DRINK

50ml (2fl oz) Hendrick's Gin
25ml (1fl oz) lime juice
10ml (¼fl oz) sugar syrup (see page 21)
6 dashes of Fee Brothers Celery
    Bitters
3 cucumber slices, plus an extra slice,
    to garnish
Fever-Tree Soda Water, to top up

In a cocktail shaker, shake all the ingredients, except the soda water, with ice cubes, then strain into a chilled highball over ice cubes. Top up with the soda water and garnish with a large cucumber slice in the drink.

Ramos Gin Fizz

MAKES 1 DRINK

50ml (2fl oz) Haymans Old Tom Gin
25ml (1fl oz) double cream
12.5ml (2½ tsp) lemon juice
12.5ml (2½ tsp) lime juice
35ml (1fl oz) sugar syrup (see page 21)
3 dashes of orange flower water
Fever-Tree Soda Water, to top up

In a cocktail shaker, dry shake all the ingredients, except the soda water. Add 3 ice cubes and shake again until they are completely dissolved. Fine-strain into a chilled highball and top up with the soda water.

✦ Credit: Henry Charles Ramos, Imperial Cabinet Saloon, New Orleans

Morning Glory Fizz

MAKES 1 DRINK

45ml (1½fl oz) Chivas Regal 12 Year Old Blended Scotch Whisky
20ml (¾fl oz) lemon juice
20ml (¾fl oz) sugar syrup (see page 21)
2 dashes of Pernod Absinthe
1 egg white
Fever-Tree Soda Water, to top up

In a cocktail shaker, dry shake all the ingredients, then add ice cubes and shake again. Strain into a chilled highball filled with ice cubes and top up with the soda water.

✦ Credit: George Winter, *How to Mix Drinks* (1884), and O H Byron, *The Modern Bartenders' Guide* (1884)

Imperial Buck

MAKES 1 DRINK

30ml (1fl oz) Gosling's Black Seal Rum
35ml (1fl oz) pineapple juice
15ml (½fl oz) lime juice
10ml (¼fl oz) Ginger Syrup (see page 195)
15ml (½fl oz) sugar syrup (see page 21)
Fever-Tree Soda Water, to top up
Pineapple slice, to garnish

In a cocktail shaker, shake all the ingredients, except the soda water, with ice cubes, then strain into a chilled highball filled with ice cubes. Top up with the soda water and garnish with a slice of pineapple.

✦ Credit: Sam Ross, Milk & Honey, New York

Peach Blow Fizz

MAKES 1 DRINK

35ml (1fl oz) Plymouth Gin
15ml (½fl oz) lemon juice
15ml (½fl oz) double cream
25ml (1fl oz) sugar syrup (see page 21)
1 egg white
2 strawberries
Fever-Tree Soda Water, to top up

In a cocktail shaker, dry shake all the ingredients, except the soda water, then add ice cubes and shake again. Fine-strain into a chilled fizz glass or highball filled with ice cubes and top up with the soda water.

Apple Blow Fizz

MAKES 1 DRINK

50ml (2fl oz) Adrien Camut 6 Year Old Calvados
20ml (¾fl oz) lemon juice
20ml (¾fl oz) sugar syrup (see page 21)
1 egg white
Fever-Tree Soda Water, to top up

In a cocktail shaker, dry shake all the ingredients, except the soda water, then add ice cubes and shake again. Strain into a chilled highball filled with ice cubes and top up with the soda water.

← Previous page, left to right
Albemarie Fizz (see page 154)
Morning Glory Fizz (see above)
Peach Blow Fizz (see above)
Chicago Fizz (see page 146)

→ Ramos Gin Fizz

Ginger Sling

MAKES 1 DRINK

50ml (2fl oz) Belvedere Vodka
15ml (½fl oz) Ginger Syrup (see
    page 195)
20ml (¾fl oz) lime juice
Fever-Tree Ginger Ale, to top up
Slice of fresh root ginger, to garnish

In a cocktail shaker, shake all the
ingredients, except the ginger ale,
with ice cubes, then fine-strain into
a chilled highball over ice cubes. Top
up with the ginger ale and garnish
with the slice of fresh ginger.

✦ Credit: Aidan Bryan, Claridge's Bar,
London

Albemarle Fizz

MAKES 1 DRINK

50ml (2fl oz) Plymouth Gin
20ml (¾fl oz) lemon juice
20ml (¾fl oz) sugar syrup (see
    page 21)
2 raspberries
Fever-Tree Soda Water, to top up

In a cocktail shaker, shake all the
ingredients, except the soda water,
with ice cubes, then fine-strain into a
chilled fizz glass or highball filled with
ice cubes and top up with the soda
water.

Missionary's Downfall

MAKES 1 DRINK

30ml (1fl oz) Bacardí Carta Blanca
    Rum
10ml (¼fl oz) Merlet Crème de Pêche
25ml (1fl oz) pineapple juice
15ml (½fl oz) lime juice
15ml (½fl oz) sugar syrup (see page 21)
5 mint leaves, plus a mint sprig, to
    garnish
10ml (¼fl oz) Wood's Navy Rum
Pineapple slice, to garnish

Churn all the ingredients, except
the navy rum, with crushed ice in a
cocktail shaker. Pour into a chilled
punch glass over crushed ice. Float
the navy rum on top and garnish with
a mint sprig and a slice of pineapple.

✦ Credit: Donn Beach, Don the
Beachcomber, Hollywood

Fog Cutter

MAKES 1 DRINK

15ml (½fl oz) Rémy Martin VSOP
    Cognac
20ml (¾fl oz) Havana Club 3 Year Old
    Rum
10ml (¼fl oz) Plymouth Gin
5ml (1 tsp) Lustau Fino Sherry
35ml (1fl oz) orange juice
12.5ml (2½ tsp) lemon juice
20ml (¾fl oz) sugar syrup (see page 21)
7.5ml (1½ tsp) Bristol Syrup Company
    Orgeat
Orange slice, to garnish
Mint sprig, to garnish

In a cocktail shaker, shake all the
ingredients with ice cubes, then
fine-strain into a chilled highball filled
with crushed ice. Garnish with a slice
of orange and a mint sprig.

✦ Credit: Trader Vic

Queens Park Swizzle

MAKES 1 DRINK

50ml (2fl oz) Havana Club Especial
    Rum
20ml (¾fl oz) lime juice
15ml (½fl oz) sugar syrup (see page 21)
8 dashes of Angostura bitters, plus a
    little extra, to garnish
8 mint leaves, plus a mint sprig, to
    garnish

Build the ingredients in a mixing tin
and churn with crushed ice. Pour into
a chilled highball and top with more
crushed ice. Garnish with a ring of
bitters around the inside of the rim,
cap with more crushed ice and finish
with a mint sprig.

✦ Credit: Queens Park Hotel, Port of Spain,
Trinidad

How to host your own cocktail party

What one experiences upon leaving Claridge's is an immediate urge to plan your return. But when this is not possible, a party in your own home can use some of the same principles that have been delighting our guests.

On any given night at Claridge's, there are not only over 700 guests in the four bars, but also up to 1,000 people across the event spaces, all in need of a cocktail. When Diane von Furstenberg designed the Claridge's Christmas Tree in 2018, there was a party to celebrate for 300 guests. Claridge's created five cocktails for the event and made 300 of each, as well as serving another five classic cocktails on request. All in all, nearly 2,100 cocktails were consumed over the course of the evening. Merry Christmas, indeed.

Whether you are making cocktails for 500, 50 or 15 people, advance planning is essential. Spend time deciding on recipes beforehand, so you can work out what spirits are needed. Consider the number of citrus fruits you need for juice and garnish: each lemon contains approximately 40ml (1½fl oz) of juice, each lime 25ml (1fl oz); and you can get four or five twists from each fruit.

As a rule, for a party of up to 50 people, there should be a choice of three drinks: one long and citrus-based, one spirits-forward and one Champagne-based.

Juices and syrups can be pre-batched. If, for example, you are serving a Moscow Mule (see page 162), mix the correct ratios of lime juice, sugar syrup and ginger syrup into one bottle, so that you can simply add 35ml (1fl oz) of this mixture to each drink when serving.

At a standalone cocktail party, allow for three drinks per person (or 1–2 if there is a dinner afterwards). Unless the intention is to get your guests somewhat befuddled, do not serve Martinis – although if you do, you will probably only need to plan for 1–2 per person.

You absolutely must have plenty of ice. You will need it for shaking, stirring and serving. To be safe, allow for 500g (1lb 2oz) of ice per drink or 1.5kg (3lb 5oz) per person.

SETTING UP

Once all the necessary pre-planning has been done, consider your set up and *mise en place*. Ideally you can commandeer a small area in the kitchen or wherever you are entertaining. Have a chopping board, knife and peeler to hand for twists and garnishes. Now, place all your bottles and tools on the left-hand side of your station. Once you have used each bottle, place it on the right-hand side. This stops you from forgetting any ingredient and allows you to check what you've added so far if you get distracted by the idle gossip of your most scurrilous friend. Take your time, jigger accurately and taste the cocktails as you go along (dip a metal straw into the drink, with your finger over the other end to trap a little liquid inside).

Once you have finished making your drinks you should clean down, wash all your tools and reset, ready for the next round.

BE PREPARED

If you'd rather spend time mingling than mixing, pre-prepared bottles of Martinis, daiquiris or White Russians (see page 115) will make life infinitely easier – and rather jollier. On the night in question, you will simply need to pour and garnish.

With bottled cocktails, the most important things to consider are dilution and temperature. As you will be serving straight from the bottle rather than stirring or shaking with ice, you need to add a small amount of still mineral water to the cocktail to adequately dilute the mixture. As a rule, you should add 10-15% of the

volume of the cocktail in water. So, in a classic Martini containing 60ml (2fl oz) gin, 12.5ml (¼fl oz) dry vermouth and a dash of orange bitters (see page44), you would add around 10ml (¼fl oz) water for dilution.

You must also keep the bottle either in the freezer (for spirit-forward drinks such as Manhattans) or, for a cocktail that contains juices or any other ingredients that would freeze, in the refrigerator.

From left to right:
Tommy's Margarita (see page 122)
Kir (see page 180)
Champagne Cocktail (see page 28)

Zombie

MAKES 1 DRINK

20ml (¾fl oz) El Dorado 15 Year Old Rum
20ml (¾fl oz) Havana Club Especial Rum
20ml (¾fl oz) Ron Zacapa 23 Centenario
20ml (¾fl oz) Bacardí Carta Blanca Rum
25ml (1fl oz) lime juice
20ml (¾fl oz) grapefruit juice
15ml (½fl oz) John D Taylor's Velvet Falernum
10ml (¼fl oz) Bristol Syrup Company Grenadine
5ml (1 tsp) Maraschino
2 dashes of Pernod Absinthe
2 dashes of Angostura bitters
Pineapple slice, to garnish
Mint sprig, to garnish

In a cocktail shaker, shake all the ingredients with ice cubes, then fine-strain into a chilled stemmed beer glass filled with crushed ice. Garnish with a slice of pineapple and a mint sprig.

✦ Credit: Donn Beach, Don the Beachcomber, Hollywood

Jungle Bird

MAKES 1 DRINK

40ml (1½fl oz) Gosling's Black Seal Rum
10ml (¼fl oz) Campari
40ml (1½fl oz) pineapple juice
15ml (½fl oz) lime juice
15ml (½fl oz) sugar syrup (see page 21)
Pineapple wedge, to garnish
4 pineapple leaves, to garnish

In a cocktail shaker, shake all the ingredients with ice cubes, then strain into a chilled rocks glass over an ice block. Garnish with a pineapple wedge and 4 pineapple leaves.

✦ Credit: Jeffrey Ong, Kuala Lumpur

Piña Colada

(blended version)

MAKES 1 DRINK

50ml (2fl oz) Bacardí Carta Blanca Rum
40ml (1½fl oz) pineapple juice
10ml (¼fl oz) lime juice
25ml (1fl oz) coconut cream
6 fresh pineapple chunks, plus a pineapple wedge, to garnish

Blend all the ingredients with a scoop of crushed ice until silky smooth. Pour into a chilled highball and garnish with a pineapple wedge on the rim of the glass.

Piña Colada

(shaken version)

MAKES 1 DRINK

40ml (1½fl oz) Bacardí Carta Blanca Rum
15ml (½fl oz) Plantation Stiggins' Fancy Pineapple Rum
40ml (1½fl oz) pineapple juice
5ml (1 tsp) lime juice
15ml (½fl oz) coconut cream
2.5ml (½ tsp) Cane Syrup (see page 194)
Mint sprig, to garnish

Whip shake all the ingredients with 3 ice cubes until they are fully dissolved, then pour into a chilled stemmed beer glass over crushed ice. Garnish with a mint sprig.

→ Left to right
Jungle Bird (see above)
Zombie (see above)
Fog Cutter (see page 154)

Batanga

MAKES 1 DRINK

Sea salt
40ml (1½fl oz) Tapatio Blanco Tequila
12.5ml (2½ tsp) lime juice
Coca-Cola, to top up
Lime wedge, to garnish

Rim a chilled highball with sea salt
(see page 19). Build the tequila and
lime juice in the glass with ice cubes.
Top up with Coca-Cola and garnish
with a lime wedge.

✦ Credit: Don Javier Delgado Corona,
La Capilla, Tequila, Mexico

1789

MAKES 1 DRINK

45ml (1½fl oz) Coffee-infused
    Plantation 3 Stars Rum (see
    page 203)
30ml (1fl oz) Dewatsuru Sakura Emaki
    Rosé Sake
25ml (1fl oz) lemon juice
15ml (½fl oz) Cane Syrup (see page
    194)
15ml (½fl oz) pineapple juice
1 egg white
Fever-Tree Mediterranean Tonic
    Water, to top up

In a cocktail shaker, dry shake all the
ingredients, except the tonic water,
then add ice cubes and shake again.
Pour into a flute and top up with the
tonic water.

✦ Credit: Harrison Ginsberg, Crown Shy,
New York

Treat for Kings

MAKES 1 DRINK

50ml (2fl oz) Ilegal Mezcal
25ml (1fl oz) lime juice
5ml (1 tsp) agave syrup
3 fresh pineapple wedges, plus an
    extra wedge, to garnish
Fever-Tree Soda Water, to top up
Mint sprig, to garnish

In a cocktail shaker, shake all the
ingredients, except the soda water,
with ice cubes, then strain into a
chilled highball filled with ice cubes.
Top up with the soda water and
garnish with a pineapple wedge and
a mint sprig.

✦ Credit: Riccardo Vacca, Claridge's Bar,
London

Chartreuse Swizzle

MAKES 1 DRINK

30ml (1fl oz) Green Chartreuse
10ml (¼fl oz) John D Taylor's Velvet
    Falernum
30ml (1fl oz) pineapple juice
10ml (¼fl oz) lime juice
Pineapple wedge, to garnish
Lime wedge, to garnish

Churn all the ingredients in a cocktail
shaker with crushed ice, then pour
into a chilled highball. Top up with
more crushed ice and garnish with a
pineapple wedge and a lime wedge.

✦ Credit: Marco Dionysos, Tres Agaves,
San Francisco

Cuba Libre

MAKES 1 DRINK

½ a lime, cut into 4 wedges, plus an
    extra wedge, to garnish
50ml (2fl oz) Havana Club 7 Year Old
    Rum
Coca-Cola, to top up

Muddle the lime wedges in a chilled
highball, until the juice and oils are
released. Add the rum and a splash
of the Coca-Cola and stir. Add
ice cubes and stir again from the
bottom of the glass. Top up with
Coca-Cola and garnish with another
lime wedge.

Mamie Taylor

MAKES 1 DRINK

50ml (2fl oz) Johnnie Walker Black
    Label Whisky
15ml (½fl oz) lime juice
10ml (¼fl oz) sugar syrup (see page 21)
10ml (¼fl oz) Ginger Syrup (see
    page 195)
Fever-Tree Ginger Ale, to top up
Lime wedge, to garnish
Crystallized ginger, to garnish

Build the ingredients, except the
ginger ale, in a chilled highball over
ice cubes. Top up with the ginger
ale. Garnish with a lime wedge and
a piece of crystallized ginger on a
cocktail stick.

✦ **Credit: Albert S Crockett,** *The Old
Waldorf-Astoria Bar Book* **(1934)**

Scorpion

MAKES 1 DRINK

25ml (1fl oz) Rémy Martin VSOP
    Cognac
25ml (1fl oz) Appleton Estate Jamaica
    Rum
25ml (1fl oz) orange juice
15ml (½fl oz) lemon juice
15ml (½fl oz) sugar syrup (see page 21)
7.5ml (1½ tsp) Bristol Syrup Company
    Orgeat
Pineapple wedge, to garnish
Fabbri Amarena cherry, to garnish

In a cocktail shaker, shake all the
ingredients with ice cubes, then fine-
strain into a chilled rocks glass over
an ice block. Garnish with a wedge
of pineapple and the cherry.

✦ **Credit: Victor Bergeron,** *Trader Vic's
Bartender's Guide* **(1947)**

Singapore Sling

MAKES 1 DRINK

40ml (1½ fl oz) Plymouth Gin
10ml (¼fl oz) Heering Cherry Liqueur
15ml (½fl oz) Cointreau
5ml (1 tsp) Bénédictine
35ml (1fl oz) pineapple juice
15ml (½fl oz) lime juice
5ml (1 tsp) Bristol Syrup Company
    Grenadine
1 dash of Angostura bitters
Fever-Tree Soda Water, to top up

TO GARNISH
Orange slice
Fabbri Amarena cherry
Mint sprig

In a cocktail shaker, shake all the
ingredients, except the soda water,
with ice cubes, then strain into a
chilled highball filled with ice cubes.
Top up with the soda water and
garnish with a slice of orange, a
cherry and a mint sprig.

✦ **Credit: Ngiam Tong Boon, Raffles Hotel,
Singapore**

Claridge's Regal

MAKES 1 DRINK

2 orange slices
2 lemon slices
½ a passionfruit
8 mint leaves, plus a mint sprig, to garnish
50ml (2fl oz) Chivas Regal 18 Year Old Blended Scotch Whisky
25ml (1fl oz) Cocchi Americano
10ml (¼fl oz) sugar syrup (see page 21)

Gently churn all the ingredients in a cocktail shaker with crushed ice. Pour into a highball and garnish with a mint sprig.

✦ Credit: Denis Broci, Claridge's Bar, London

Gin Gin Mule

MAKES 1 DRINK

50ml (2fl oz) Beefeater London Dry Gin
20ml (¾fl oz) lime juice
10ml (¼fl oz) Ginger Syrup (see page 195)
15ml (½fl oz) sugar syrup (see page 21)
4 mint leaves, plus a mint sprig, to garnish
Fever-Tree Soda Water, to top up
Lime wedge, to garnish

In a cocktail shaker, shake all the ingredients, except the soda water, with ice cubes. Strain into a chilled highball filled with ice cubes. Top up with the soda water and garnish with a mint sprig and a lime wedge.

✦ Credit: Audrey Saunders, Pegu Club, New York

Moscow Mule

MAKES 1 DRINK

50ml (2fl oz) Belvedere Vodka
15ml (½fl oz) lime juice
10ml (¼fl oz) sugar syrup (see page 21)
10ml (¼fl oz) Ginger Syrup (see page 195)
2 dashes of Angostura bitters, plus 2 extra dashes, to garnish
Fentimans Ginger Beer, to top up
Lime wedge, to garnish

In a cocktail shaker, shake all the ingredients, except the ginger beer, with ice cubes, then strain into a chilled highball filled with ice cubes. Top up with the ginger beer and garnish with 2 dashes of bitters and a lime wedge.

✦ Credit: Wes Price, Cock 'n' Bull, Hollywood

Mojito

MAKES 1 DRINK

50ml (2fl oz) Bacardí Ron Superior Heritage Limited Edition or Havana Club Especial Rum
20ml (¾fl oz) lime juice
20ml (¾fl oz) sugar syrup (see page 21)
8 mint leaves, plus a mint sprig, to garnish
Lime wedge, to garnish

Churn all the ingredients in a cocktail shaker with crushed ice, then pour into a chilled highball. Top up with more crushed ice and garnish with a mint sprig and a lime wedge.

Smokey Cokey

MAKES 1 DRINK

35ml (1fl oz) Lagavulin 16 Year Old Whisky
Coca-Cola, to top up

Build the whisky in a chilled highball over ice cubes. Top up with Coca-Cola, then stir to combine.

Añejo Highball

MAKES 1 DRINK

40ml (1½fl oz) Havana Club 7 Year
     Old Rum
25ml (1fl oz) Pierre Ferrand Dry
     Curaçao
2 dashes of Angostura bitters
5ml (1 tsp) lime juice
Fentimans Ginger Beer, to top up
Orange slice, to garnish

In a cocktail shaker, shake all the
ingredients, except the ginger beer,
with ice cubes. Strain into a chilled
highball filled with ice cubes. Top up
with the ginger beer and garnish with
a slice of orange.

✦ Credit: Dale DeGroff, The Rainbow Room,
New York

Grapefruit Americano

MAKES 1 DRINK

25ml (1fl oz) Campari
25ml (1fl oz) Martini Rosso
25ml (1fl oz) Grapefruit Cordial (see
     page 192)
2 dashes of Saline Solution (see
     page 210)
Fever-Tree Soda Water, to top up
Pink grapefruit slice, to garnish

Build all the ingredients, except the
soda water, in a chilled highball filled
with ice cubes. Top up with the soda
water and garnish with a slice of pink
grapefruit.

✦ Credit: Darren Leaney, Capitano,
Melbourne

Northern Soul

MAKES 1 DRINK

25ml (1fl oz) Ketel One Vodka
25ml (1fl oz) Aperol
20ml (¾fl oz) lime juice
5ml (1 tsp) sugar syrup (see page 21)
4 dashes of Fee Brothers Rhubarb
     Bitters
Fentimans Ginger Beer, to top up

TO GARNISH
Orange twist
Crystallized ginger
Cinnamon stick

In a cocktail shaker, shake all the
ingredients, except the ginger beer,
with ice cubes, then strain into a
chilled highball filled with ice cubes.
Top up with the ginger beer and
garnish with an orange twist, a piece
of crystallized ginger on a cocktail
stick and a cinnamon stick.

✦ Credit: Andreas Cortes, Claridge's Bar,
London

Fish House Punch

MAKES 1 DRINK

30ml (1fl oz) Rémy Martin VSOP
     Cognac
30ml (1fl oz) Gosling's Black Seal Rum
10ml (¼fl oz) Merlet Crème de Pêche
20ml (¾fl oz) lemon juice
15ml (½fl oz) sugar syrup (see page 21)

TO GARNISH
Lemon wedge
Mint sprig
Grated nutmeg

In a cocktail shaker, shake all the
ingredients with ice cubes, then
strain into a chilled highball over
crushed ice. Garnish with a lemon
wedge, a mint sprig and a little
grated nutmeg.

Paloma

MAKES 1 DRINK

Sea salt
50ml (2fl oz) Tapatio Blanco Tequila
25ml (1fl oz) grapefruit juice
10ml (¼fl oz) lime juice
15ml (½fl oz) sugar syrup (see page 21)
Three Cents Pink Grapefruit Soda, to top up
Lime wedge, to garnish

Half-rim a chilled highball with sea salt (see page 19). In a cocktail shaker, shake all the ingredients, except the soda, with ice cubes. Strain into the glass over ice cubes, then top up with the soda and garnish with a lime wedge.

✦ Made popular by: Don Javier Delgado Corona, La Capilla, Tequila, Mexico

Dark & Stormy

MAKES 1 DRINK

50ml (2fl oz) Gosling's Black Seal Rum
15ml (½fl oz) lime juice
10ml (¼fl oz) Ginger Syrup (see page 195)
5ml (1 tsp) sugar syrup (see page 21)
Fentimans Ginger Beer, to top up
Lime wedge, to garnish
Crystallized ginger, to garnish

Build the ingredients, except the ginger beer, in a chilled highball over ice cubes. Top up with the ginger beer. Garnish with a lime wedge and a piece of crystallized ginger on a cocktail stick.

✦ The National Drink of Bermuda

Saratoga Brace Up

MAKES 1 DRINK

45ml (1½fl oz) Rémy Martin VSOP Cognac
20ml (¾fl oz) lemon juice
20ml (¾fl oz) sugar syrup (see page 21)
2 dashes of Pernod Absinthe
1 egg white
Fever-Tree Soda Water, to top up

In a cocktail shaker, dry shake all the ingredients, except the soda water, then add ice cubes and shake again. Strain into a chilled highball filled with ice cubes and top up with the soda water.

✦ Credit: *Jerry Thomas' Bartenders Guide* (1862)

Pear Shandy

MAKES 1 DRINK

75ml (2½fl oz) Lustau Amontillado Sherry
15ml (½fl oz) St George Spiced Pear Liqueur
15ml (½fl oz) lemon juice
15ml (½fl oz) Cinnamon Bark Syrup (see page 195)
5ml (1 tsp) sugar syrup (see page 21)
2 pear slices
75ml (2½fl oz) Burning Sky Arise Pale Ale

In a cocktail shaker, shake all the ingredients, except the pear slices and pale ale, with ice cubes. Place the pear slices in a chilled highball, add the pale ale and then fine-strain in the shaken cocktail.

✦ Credit: Pietro Collina, Davies and Brook, London

Gentlemen's Buck

MAKES 1 DRINK

40ml (1½fl oz) Michter's US*1 Kentucky Straight Rye Whiskey
35ml (1fl oz) pineapple juice
15ml (½fl oz) lime juice
10ml (¼fl oz) Ginger Syrup (see page 195)
15ml (½fl oz) sugar syrup (see page 21)
Fever-Tree Soda Water, to top up
Pineapple slice, to garnish

In a cocktail shaker, shake all the ingredients, except the soda water, with ice cubes, then strain into a chilled highball filled with ice cubes. Top up with the soda water and garnish with a slice of pineapple.

Sloe Passion

MAKES 1 DRINK

30ml (1fl oz) Plymouth Sloe Gin
20ml (¾fl oz) Tanqueray London Dry
    Gin
125ml (4fl oz) pineapple juice
10ml (¼fl oz) lemon juice
½ a passionfruit, plus another ½,
    to garnish

In a cocktail shaker, shake all the
ingredients with ice cubes, then
strain into a chilled highball filled
with ice cubes. Garnish with half a
passionfruit.

✦ Credit: Tina Bryan, Claridge's Bar, London

El Diablo

MAKES 1 DRINK

50ml (2fl oz) Tapatio Blanco Tequila
15ml (½fl oz) lime juice
10ml (¼fl oz) Ginger Syrup (see
    page 195)
5ml (1 tsp) sugar syrup (see page 21)
Fever-Tree Ginger Ale, to top up
5ml (1 tsp) Merlet Crème de Cassis
Lime wedge, to garnish

Build the first 4 ingredients in a
chilled highball over ice cubes. Top
up with the ginger ale. Float the
crème de cassis on top and garnish
with a lime wedge.

✦ Credit: *Trader Vic's Book of Food & Drink*
(1946)

That's Life

MAKES 1 DRINK

40ml (1½ fl oz) Monkey Shoulder
    Scotch Whisky
10ml (¼fl oz) Ilegal Joven Mezcal
25ml (1fl oz) Cocchi Barolo Chinato
10ml (¼fl oz) Salted Lapsang Syrup
    (see page 196)
Fever-Tree Soda Water, to top up
2 large capers, to garnish

Stir all the ingredients, except the
soda water, in a mixing glass, then
strain into a chilled highball over a
long ice block. Top up with the soda
water and garnish with the capers.

✦ Credit: Declan McGurk, The Savoy,
London

Hoffman House Fizz

MAKES 1 DRINK

35ml (1fl oz) Plymouth Gin
15ml (½fl oz) lemon juice
15ml (½fl oz) sugar syrup (see page 21)
15ml (½fl oz) double cream
1 egg white
5ml (1 tsp) Bristol Syrup Company
    Grenadine
1 orange slice
Fever-Tree Soda Water, to top up

In a cocktail shaker, dry shake all the
ingredients, except the soda water.
Add ice cubes, then shake again.
Strain into a chilled highball filled
with ice cubes and top up with the
soda water.

✦ Credit: David A Embury, *The Fine Art
of Mixing Drinks* (1948)

Presbyterian

MAKES 1 DRINK

50ml (2fl oz) Michter's US*1 Kentucky
    Straight Rye Whiskey
15ml (½fl oz) lime juice
10ml (¼fl oz) sugar syrup (see page 21)
10ml (¼fl oz) Ginger Syrup (see
    page 195)
Fever-Tree Ginger Ale, to top up
Orange slice, to garnish

Build the ingredients, except the
ginger ale, in a chilled highball. Top
up with the ginger ale and garnish
with a slice of orange.

No & Low

← Adonis (see page 180)

Claridge's Cocktail Hour

Claridge's is firmly of the opinion that Cocktail Hour is any hour you please.

The Bright Young Things of the 1920s considered 'Cocktail Hour' to last from 5.30pm to 7pm. This is according to Alec Waugh, brother of Evelyn, who claimed to have invented the cocktail party here in London. A drinks party before dinner, rather than after as was customary, seemed like a far superior idea for all concerned. Thus, in the autumn of 1925, Waugh invited 30 guests to a late afternoon tea with 'the conventional appurtenances of a tea: crumpets, cakes, savoury sandwiches ... Then, at a quarter to six, I produced my surprise – a beaker of Daiquiris.' Guest and bestselling novelist Sheila Kaye-Smith was unable to make her dinner date, the word spread, and the Cocktail Hour was born.

At Claridge's, the Cocktail Hour stretches boundlessly. Pineapple daiquiris are shaken and mandarin negronis stirred from noon until the early hours. While the bars tend to be busiest around 6pm as guests flock in for a restorative pre-dinner pick me up – if you would like a Flapper at 11am, an Apple Collins at 3pm or a 1am Mary Pickford, then by all means be our guest.

The Painter's Room, which opened in 2021, was designed precisely with the ethos that any hour can be Cocktail Hour. It takes inspiration from the Continental culture of lighter drinks, consumed whenever the fancy takes. Thus, drinks in The Painter's Room veer towards the long and spritzy, the fizzy and fragrant: approachable drinks such as the Nishi (see page 178) and Golden Hour (see page 181). These are drinks that liven rather than lull and tempt rather than quash the appetite. At Claridge's, a cocktail is never out of the question – regardless of the hour.

Aperol Spritz

MAKES 1 DRINK

100ml (3½fl oz) Laurent-Perrier La Cuvée NV Champagne
20ml (¾fl oz) Fever-Tree Soda Water
50ml (2fl oz) Aperol
Orange slice, to garnish

Build the ingredients in a wine glass, in the order above to reduce the loss of carbonation. Add ice cubes with tongs and stir lightly to combine. Garnish with a slice of orange.

Diplomat

MAKES 1 DRINK

35ml (1fl oz) Martini Bianco
35ml (1fl oz) Martini Rosso
7.5ml (1½ tsp) Maraschino
2 dashes of orange bitters
1 dash of Angostura bitters

Lightly stir all the ingredients in a mixing glass, then pour into a chilled coupe.

✦ **Credit: Harry Craddock, American Bar, The Savoy, London**

Corgi Spritz

MAKES 1 DRINK

30ml (1fl oz) Aperol
30ml (1fl oz) Cocchi Americano
5ml (1 tsp) Bristol Syrup Company Passionfruit
2.5ml (½ tsp) sugar
Three Cents Pink Grapefruit Soda, to top up
Orange twist, to garnish

In a cocktail shaker, shake all the ingredients, except the soda, with ice cubes, then fine-strain into a chilled short stemmed wine glass. Top up with the soda and garnish with an orange twist.

✦ **Adapted by: Matteo Carretta, Davies and Brook, London**

Poire Normandie

MAKES 1 DRINK

40ml (1½fl oz) Poire Normandie Batch (see page 205)
40ml (1½fl oz) Eric Bordelet Poiré Authentique
10ml (¼fl oz) sugar syrup (see page 21)
1 dash of Citric Acid Solution (see page 210)
Green apple slice, to garnish

Stir all the ingredients in a mixing glass with ice cubes, then strain into a chilled rocks glass over an ice block. Garnish with the green apple slice.

✦ **Credit: Nathan McCarley-O'Neill, The Painter's Room, London**

Milano Torino

MAKES 1 DRINK

35ml (1fl oz) Campari
35ml (1fl oz) Carpano Antica Formula Vermouth
Orange coin, to garnish

Build the Campari and vermouth in a chilled rocks glass over an ice block. Stir for 10–15 seconds, then garnish with an orange coin.

→ Overleaf, left to right
Diplomat (see above)
Milano Torino (see above)
Corgi Spritz (see above)
Aperol Spritz (see above)
Rome with a View (see page 176)

Menthe

MAKES 1 DRINK

25ml (1fl oz) Peppermint & Lemon
    Cordial (see page 193)
10ml (¼fl oz) lemon juice
130ml (4½fl oz) sparkling grape
    juice (we use Château de La
    Magdeleine Perlant de Raisin
    Blanc)
Mint sprig, to garnish

Build the ingredients in a chilled wine glass over ice cubes. Garnish with a mint sprig.

Pimm's Cup

MAKES 1 DRINK

50ml (2fl oz) Pimm's No 1 Cup
1 dash of Angostura bitters
Fever-Tree Ginger Ale, to top up

TO GARNISH
Orange wedge
Lemon slice
Cucumber slice
½ a strawberry
Mint sprig

Build the Pimm's and bitters in a chilled highball filled with ice cubes, then top up with the ginger ale. Garnish with an orange wedge, a slice of lemon, a slice of cucumber, half a strawberry and a mint sprig.

Orange Flower

MAKES 1 DRINK

40ml (1½fl oz) Seedlip Spice 94
25ml (1fl oz) Æcorn Bitter
20ml (¾fl oz) lime juice
5ml (1 tsp) sugar syrup (see page 21)
5ml (1 tsp) orange flower water
Orange coin, to garnish

In a cocktail shaker, shake all the ingredients with ice cubes, then strain into a chilled coupe. Garnish with an orange coin.

Pear Passion

MAKES 1 DRINK

175ml (6fl oz) apple juice
20ml (¾fl oz) pear purée
15ml (½ fl oz) lime juice
½ a passionfruit, plus another ½, to
    garnish

Build all the ingredients in a chilled highball over crushed ice, then churn. Top up with more crushed ice and garnish with half a passionfruit.

Claridge's Lemonade

MAKES 1 DRINK

2 lemons, skin and pith removed, plus
    a lemon twist, to garnish
30ml (1fl oz) sugar syrup (see page 21)
200ml (7fl oz) still water

Blend all the ingredients with a small scoop of crushed ice until silky smooth. Fine-strain into a chilled highball and garnish with a lemon twist.

→ Claridge's Lemonade

La Pappa Reale

MAKES 1 DRINK

30ml (1fl oz) Suze
10ml (¼fl oz) Yellow Chartreuse
20ml (¾fl oz) Heather Honey Syrup
(see page 194)
Lemon coin, to garnish

In a cocktail shaker, dry shake all the ingredients, then hard shake with ice cubes until the shaker is very cold. Strain into a chilled half coupe. Express the lemon coin over the top, then discard.

Claridge's Garibaldi

MAKES 1 DRINK

40ml (1½fl oz) Campari
60ml (2fl oz) orange juice
10ml (¼fl oz) lime juice
10ml (¼fl oz) sugar syrup (see page 21)
5ml (1 tsp) passionfruit syrup
Orange wedge, to garnish

In a cocktail shaker, dry shake all the ingredients, then short shake with 3 ice cubes. Fine-strain into a chilled highball filled with ice cubes and garnish with an orange wedge.

✦ Credit: Matteo Carretta, Claridge's Bar, London

Rome with a View

MAKES 1 DRINK

25ml (1fl oz) Dolin Dry Vermouth
25ml (1fl oz) Campari
15ml (½fl oz) lime juice
20ml (¾fl oz) sugar syrup (see page 21)
Fever-Tree Soda Water, to top up
Orange wedge, to garnish

Build the ingredients, except the soda water, in a chilled highball filled with ice cubes. Top up with the soda water and garnish with an orange wedge.

✦ Credit: Michael McIlroy, Attaboy, New York

Sherry Cobbler

MAKES 1 DRINK

2 fresh pineapple chunks
2 orange slices, plus an orange wedge, to garnish
2 lemon wedges, plus an extra wedge, to garnish
60ml (2fl oz) Lustau Fino Sherry
15ml (½fl oz) Pierre Ferrand Dry Curaçao
10ml (¼fl oz) sugar syrup (see page 21)
15ml (½fl oz) Palo Cortado sherry

Muddle the fruit in a cocktail shaker, then add the remaining ingredients, except the Palo Cortado, and shake with ice cubes. Pour into a chilled highball over crushed ice and float the Palo Cortado on top. Garnish with orange and lemon wedges and a straw.

Soft Garibaldi

MAKES 1 DRINK

50ml (2fl oz) Æcorn Bitter
100ml (3½fl oz) orange juice
30ml (1fl oz) Heather Honey Syrup
(see page 194)
Blood orange slice, to garnish

In a cocktail shaker, shake all the ingredients with ice cubes, then fine-strain into a flute. Garnish with a slice of blood orange.

Ma Cherie

MAKES 1 DRINK

70ml (2½fl oz) Lustau Fino Sherry
15ml (½fl oz) Pineapple Cordial (see page 192)
15ml (½fl oz) lime juice
7.5ml (1½ tsp) John D Taylor's Velvet Falernum
7.5ml (1½ tsp) Green Chartreuse
2 pinches of salt
2.5cm (1 in) celery slice
1 cucumber slice, plus a cucumber ribbon, to garnish

In a cocktail shaker, lightly shake all the ingredients with ice cubes for 3–4 seconds. Fine-strain into a chilled highball with a cucumber ribbon wrapped inside the glass, over crushed ice.

✦ Credit: Leo Robitschek, NoMad Hotel, New York

Beetroot Lassi

MAKES 1 DRINK

75ml (2½fl oz) pink grapefruit juice
30ml (1fl oz) Greek yogurt
10ml (¼fl oz) lime juice
10ml (¼fl oz) agave syrup
10ml (¼fl oz) beetroot juice
Grated lime zest, to garnish

In a cocktail shaker, shake all the ingredients, except the beetroot juice, with ice cubes, then fine-strain into a chilled highball over crushed ice. Float the beetroot juice on top, add more crushed ice and then garnish with grated lime zest.

Aperol Chiaro

MAKES 1 DRINK

50ml (2fl oz) Aperol
10ml (¼fl oz) Yellow Chartreuse
4 dashes of orange bitters
Olive, to garnish

In a cocktail shaker, shake all the ingredients with ice cubes until the shaker is too cold to hold. Fine-strain into a chilled half coupe and garnish with an olive.

Nishi

MAKES 1 DRINK

75ml (2½fl oz) Nishi Batch (see page 206)
7.5ml (1½ tsp) St Lawrence Gold Pure Maple Syrup
1 dash of orange bitters

Build the ingredients in a chilled highball over an ice block. Stir for 5 seconds.

✦ Credit: Nathan McCarley-O'Neill, Davies and Brook, London

Strawberry & Vinegar

MAKES 1 DRINK

30ml (1fl oz) Cocchi Barolo Chinato
30ml (1fl oz) Merlet Crème de Fraise
    des Bois
5ml (1 tsp) aged balsamic vinegar
Orange coin, to garnish

Stir all the ingredients in a mixing
glass, with ice cubes, then strain
into a chilled half coupe. Express
the orange coin over the top, then
discard.

Pimm's & Lemonade

MAKES 1 DRINK

50ml (2fl oz) Pimm's No 1 Cup
1 dash of Angostura bitters
Fever-Tree Sicilian Lemonade,
    to top up

TO GARNISH
Orange wedge
Lemon slice
Cucumber slice
½ a strawberry
Mint sprig

Build the Pimm's and bitters into a
chilled highball filled with ice cubes,
then top up with the lemonade.
Garnish with an orange wedge, a
slice of lemon, a slice of cucumber,
half a strawberry and a mint sprig.

Adonis

MAKES 1 DRINK

60ml (2fl oz) Lustau Fino Sherry
30ml (1fl oz) sweet vermouth
2 dashes of orange bitters
Lemon twist, to garnish

Stir all the ingredients in a mixing
glass, then fine-strain into a chilled
coupe. Garnish with a lemon twist.

Spice 94

MAKES 1 DRINK

4 raspberries
50ml (2fl oz) Seedlip Spice 94
100ml (3½fl oz) apple juice
25ml (1fl oz) lemon juice
15ml (½fl oz) Heather Honey Syrup
    (see page 194)
1 egg white
Orange wedge, to garnish
Lemon wedge, to garnish

Muddle the raspberries in a cocktail
shaker, then add the remaining
ingredients and dry shake. Add ice
cubes and shake again. Pour into
a chilled highball over crushed ice
and garnish with orange and lemon
wedges and a straw.

Kir

MAKES 1 DRINK

15ml (½fl oz) Merlet Crème de Cassis
160ml (5½fl oz) dry white wine (we
    use Château La Coste Les Pentes
    Douces 2018)

Build the crème de cassis and wine
in a white wine glass over ice cubes.
Stir for 20 seconds to chill.

Banana & Fino

MAKES 1 DRINK

60ml (2fl oz) Lustau Fino Sherry
20ml (¾fl oz) Tempus Fugit Crème de
    Banane

Build the sherry and crème de
banane in a chilled rocks glass over
an ice block. Stir to chill.

✦ **Credit: Remy Savage, A Bar With Shapes
For A Name, London**

Campari Spritz

MAKES 1 DRINK

40ml (1½fl oz) Laurent-Perrier La
    Cuvée NV Champagne
35ml (1fl oz) Fever-Tree Soda Water
50ml (2fl oz) Campari
Orange slice, to garnish

Build the ingredients in a chilled
wine glass, in the order above to
reduce the loss of carbonation. Add
ice cubes with tongs and stir lightly
to combine. Garnish with a slice of
orange.

Golden Hour

MAKES 1 DRINK

30ml (1fl oz) Suze
30ml (1fl oz) St-Germain elderflower
    liqueur
60ml (2fl oz) Apple Citrus (see
    page 214)
5ml (1 tsp) sugar syrup (see page 21)
6 mint leaves
Fever-Tree Soda Water, to top up

Build all the ingredients, except the
soda water, in a chilled highball over
ice cubes. Stir, then top up with the
soda water.

✦ Credit: Nathan McCarley-O'Neill,
The Painter's Room, London

Almost A Bellini

MAKES 4 DRINKS

200ml (7fl oz) Château La Coste Rosé
100ml (3½fl oz) Pierre Ferrand Pineau
    Des Charentes
10ml (¼fl oz) Merlet Crème De Pêche
30g (1oz) caster sugar
120ml (4fl oz) water
4ml (¾tsp) Citric Acid Solution (see
    page 210)
6 dashes of Saline Solution (see
    page 210)

Combine all the ingredients in a
bottle and carbonate using a soda
syphon (use 2 charges). Leave to
rest in the refrigerator for 2 hours.
This will keep in the refrigerator for
4 weeks.

To serve, pour into a chilled wine
glass over an ice block and stir briefly.

✦ Credit: Nathan McCarley-O'Neill,
The Painter's Room, London

Pine Americano

MAKES 1 DRINK

25ml (1fl oz) Campari
25ml (1fl oz) Martini Rosso
150ml (5fl oz) Idyll Pine Forest Soda

Build the Campari and vermouth in
a chilled highball filled with ice cubes.
Top up with the soda.

✦ Credit: Marcis Dzelzainis, Idyll Drinks

Calvados & Tonic

MAKES 1 DRINK

50ml (2fl oz) Adrien Camut 6 Year Old
    Calvados
Fever-Tree Premium Indian Tonic
    Water, to top up
Lemon wedge, to garnish

Build the Calvados in a chilled
highball over ice cubes, then top
up with the tonic water. Use a bar
spoon to stir gently. Garnish with
a lemon wedge.

→ Overleaf, left to right
    The Painter's Room Old Fashioned
      (see page 62)
    Atlantic Nights (see page 84)
    Clave (see page 48)
    Honey & Chamomile (see page 44)
    Almost a Bellini (see above)
    Golden Hour (see above)

Cubano Americano

MAKES 1 DRINK

20ml (¾fl oz) **Coffee-infused Bitter Vermouth (see page 202)**
20ml (¾fl oz) **Rooibos-infused Martini Rubino (see page 205)**
15ml (½fl oz) **Bacardí Ron Superior Heritage Limited Edition**
10ml (¼fl oz) **Punt e Mes Vermouth**
35ml (1fl oz) **Fever-Tree Premium Indian Tonic Water**

Build all the ingredients, except the tonic water, in a chilled rocks glass over an ice block and stir for 20 seconds. Add the tonic water and stir for another 20 seconds.

✦ **Adapted by: Nathan McCarley-O'Neill, The Painter's Room, London**

Café Americano

MAKES 1 DRINK

40ml (1½fl oz) **Cocchi Storico Vermouth Di Torino**
15ml (½fl oz) **Mr Black Cold Brew Coffee Liqueur**
10ml (¼fl oz) **Fernet-Branca**
Fever-Tree Premium Indian Tonic Water, to top up
Orange slice, to garnish

Build the ingredients, except the tonic water, in a chilled highball over ice cubes, then top up with the tonic water. Use a bar spoon to stir gently. Garnish with a slice of orange.

Americano

MAKES 1 DRINK

35ml (1fl oz) **Campari**
35ml (1fl oz) **Carpano Antica Formula Vermouth**
Fever-Tree Soda Water, to top up
Orange slice, to garnish

Build the Campari and the vermouth in a chilled highball over ice cubes. Top up with the soda water and garnish with a slice of orange.

Atlantic Avenue

MAKES 1 DRINK

50ml (2fl oz) **Atlantic Avenue Batch (see page 201)**
15ml (½fl oz) **Rhubarb Syrup (see page 196)**
20ml (¾fl oz) **Apple Citrus (see page 214)**
2 dashes of **Cosmo Bitters (see page 214)**
Grapefruit coin, to garnish

Stir all the ingredients in a mixing glass with ice cubes for 20 seconds, then fine-strain into a chilled coupe. Garnish with a grapefruit coin.

✦ **Credit: Nathan McCarley-O'Neill, The Painter's Room, London**

White Port & Tonic

MAKES 1 DRINK

50ml (2fl oz) **Graham's Fine White Port**
Fever-Tree Premium Indian Tonic Water, to top up
Lemon wedge, to garnish
Bay leaf, to garnish

Build the port in a chilled highball over ice cubes, then top up with the tonic water. Use a bar spoon to stir gently. Garnish with a lemon wedge and a bay leaf – slap the bay leaf in the palm of your hand first, to wake it up and release the aroma and oils.

Jasmine

MAKES 1 DRINK

30ml (1fl oz) Muyu Jasmine Verte
20ml (¾fl oz) Tío Pepe Sherry
1 dash of Amargo Chuncho Bitters

Stir all the ingredients in a mixing glass with ice cubes. Strain into a chilled coupe.

✦ Credit: Monica Berg & Alex Kratena, Tayēr + Elementary, London

Nashi Pear Spritz

(Davies and Brook)

MAKES 1 DRINK

4 dashes Muyu Vetiver Gris
20ml (¾fl oz) Martini Riserva Speciale Ambrato
30ml (1fl oz) St-Germain elderflower liqueur
90ml (3fl oz) Nashi Pear Juice Reduction (see page 212)
50ml (2fl oz) Billecart-Salmon Champagne Brut Rosé
Mint sprig, to garnish

Stir all the ingredients, except the Champagne, in a mixing glass with ice cubes. Strain into a stemmed Pilsner glass over ice cubes and top up with the Champagne. Garnish with a mint sprig.

Bamboo

MAKES 1 DRINK

35ml (1fl oz) Lustau Fino Sherry
35ml (1fl oz) Dolin Dry Vermouth
5ml (1 tsp) sugar syrup (see page 21)
2 dashes of orange bitters
1 dash of Angostura bitters
Orange coin, to garnish
Fabbri Amarena cherry, to garnish

Stir all the ingredients in a mixing glass, then strain into a chilled coupe. Express the orange coin over the top, then discard. Garnish with the cherry.

✦ Credit: Louis Eppinger, Grand Hotel, Yokohama

Hugo Spritz

MAKES 1 DRINK

125ml (4fl oz) Laurent-Perrier La Cuvée NV Champagne
50ml (2fl oz) St-Germain elderflower liqueur
6 mint leaves, plus a mint sprig, to garnish
Lemon wedge, to garnish

Build the ingredients in a chilled highball, in the order above to reduce the loss of carbonation. Add ice cubes with tongs and stir lightly to combine. Garnish with a mint sprig and a lemon wedge.

Monte Flip

MAKES 1 DRINK

30ml (1fl oz) Amaro Montenegro
30ml (1fl oz) Mr Black Cold Brew Coffee Liqueur
1 egg yolk

Blitz the ingredients in a blender with 3 ice cubes for 10 seconds. Pour into a chilled coupe.

→ Nashi Pear Spritz

Keystone Snap

MAKES 1 DRINK

35ml (1fl oz) Æcorn Bitter
5ml (1 tsp) Melipona honey
50ml (2fl oz) Malawi Antlers Tea (see
    page 213)
Pink grapefruit slice, to garnish

In a cocktail shaker, shake all the
ingredients with ice cubes, then
fine-strain into a chilled coupe.
Garnish with a slice of pink grapefruit.

✦ Credit: Ryan Chetiyawardana, Mr Lyan,
London

Vermouth & Tonic

MAKES 1 DRINK

50ml (2fl oz) Cocchi Americano
Fever-Tree Premium Indian Tonic
    Water, to top up
Lemon wedge, to garnish

Build the vermouth in a chilled
highball over ice cubes, then top up
with the tonic water. Use a bar spoon
to stir gently. Garnish with a lemon
wedge.

Campari Shakerato

MAKES 1 DRINK

50ml (2fl oz) Campari
10ml (¼fl oz) liquid from a jar
    of bourbon Fabbri Amarena
    cherries
Orange coin, to garnish

In a cocktail shaker, shake the
Campari and cherry liquid with ice
cubes until the shaker is too cold to
hold – this is important to ensure
adequate dilution. The drink should
have a soft texture and be light pink
in colour. Fine-strain into a chilled
half coupe. Express the orange coin
over the top, then discard.

Claridge's Strawberry

MAKES 1 DRINK

1 cucumber slice
5ml (1tsp) Caramel Syrup (see
    page 198)
15ml (½fl oz) lemon juice
20ml (¾fl oz) D&B Strawberry Syrup
    (see page 198)
20ml (¾fl oz) Rooibos Tea (see
    page 213)
20ml (¾fl oz) Tío Pepe Dos Palmas
    Fino Sherry
20ml (¾fl oz) Aperol
25ml (1fl oz) Monkey 47 Gin
25ml (1fl oz) London Essence Co.
    Grapefruit & Rosemary Tonic
    Water
Basil leaf, to garnish

In a cocktail shaker, shake all the
ingredients, except the tonic water,
with ice cubes, then fine-strain into a
chilled rocks glass over an ice block.
Top up with tonic water and garnish
with a basil leaf.

VP&T

MAKES 1 DRINK

30ml (1fl oz) Pommeau de Normandie
15ml (½fl oz) Vine Leaf-infused
    Tanqueray No Ten (see page 206)
2.5ml (½ tsp) sugar syrup (see
    page 21)
Schweppes Tonic Water, to top up
Skeleton leaf, to garnish

Build the ingredients, except the
tonic water, in a chilled highball over
ice cubes, then top up with the tonic
water. Use a bar spoon to stir gently.
Garnish with a skeleton leaf.

✦ Credit: Daniel Schofield, Schofield's Bar,
Manchester

➔ Claridge's Strawberry

Shrubs, Cordials, Syrups & Tinctures

Shrubs

Mandarin Shrub

MAKES 1 LITRE (1¾ PINT)

500ml (18fl oz) mandarin juice
400g (14oz) caster sugar
100ml (3½fl oz) white wine vinegar
Rind of 6 mandarins

Combine all the ingredients in a vacuum bag and sous-vide at 60°C (140°F) for 30 minutes.

Rest in an ice bath for 10 minutes, then pass through a paper coffee filter into a large bottle. This will keep in the refrigerator for up to 2 weeks.

Raspberry Shrub

MAKES 1 LITRE (1¾ PINT)

250g (9oz) fresh raspberries
400ml (14fl oz) still mineral water
100ml (3½fl oz) reserve sherry vinegar
500g (1lb 2oz) caster sugar

Combine the raspberries, the measured water and the vinegar in a saucepan over a low heat until the water has taken on the colour of the raspberries. Add the sugar and continue to heat for another 5 minutes until the sugar has completely dissolved.

Pass through a chinois into a large bottle. This will keep in the refrigerator for up to 4 weeks.

Pomelo Shrub

MAKES 800ML (27FL OZ)

500ml (18fl oz) pomelo juice
500g (1lb 2oz) caster sugar

Combine the pomelo juice and sugar in a saucepan over a low heat and simmer until the sugar has dissolved. Remove from the heat and leave to cool.

Once the liquid is room temperature, pour into a bottle. This will keep in the refrigerator for up to 4 weeks.

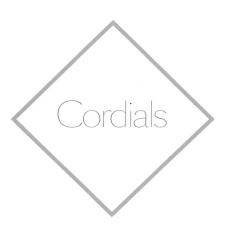

Cordials

Olive Leaf Cordial

MAKES 760ML (26½FL OZ)

200ml (7fl oz) warm water
130g (4½oz) caster sugar
10g (¼oz) fresh olive leaf
5g (⅛oz) citric acid powder
350ml (12fl oz) OP Anderson Aquavit
115ml (4fl oz) Æcorn Aperitif Dry

Combine the measured water with the sugar, olive leaf and citric acid and leave to infuse for 4 hours.

Add the aquavit and Æcorn. Pass through a chinois into a large bottle. This will keep in the refrigerator for up to 4 weeks.

Grapefruit Cordial

MAKES 850ML (1½ PINT)

24g (1oz) white grapefruit rind
240g (8½oz) caster sugar
600ml (20fl oz) white grapefruit juice
12g (½oz) citric acid powder

Combine the grapefruit rind and sugar and leave to infuse for 30 minutes.

Remove the rind from the sugar and stir in the grapefruit juice. Once the sugar has dissolved, add the citric acid and mix again.

Pour into a large bottle. This will keep in the refrigerator for up to 4 weeks.

Pear Cordial

MAKES 730ML (1⅓ PINTS)

150g (5½oz) Passe Crassane pear, diced, skin left on
6g (¼oz) malic acid powder
5g (⅛oz) citric acid powder
360ml (12½fl oz) still mineral water
210g (7½oz) caster sugar

Combine all the ingredients in a vacuum bag and leave to infuse for 24 hours.

Pass through a paper coffee filter into a bottle. This will keep in the refrigerator for up to 4 weeks.

Pineapple Cordial

MAKES 500ML (18FL OZ)

250ml (9fl oz) pineapple juice
250g (9oz) caster sugar
5g (⅛oz) citric acid powder

Blitz all the ingredients in a blender, then pass through a chinois into a bottle. This will keep in the refrigerator for up to 4 weeks.

Parsnip & Thyme Cordial

MAKES 600ML (20FL OZ)

200g (7oz) parsnips, peeled and diced
20g (¾oz) dried Greek thyme
400ml (14fl oz) still mineral water
200g (7oz) caster sugar
6g (¼oz) citric acid powder

Combine the parsnips, thyme and measured water in a vacuum bag. Sous-vide at 60°C (140°F) for 1 hour.

Pass through a paper coffee filter, then add the sugar and citric acid. Stir until the sugar has dissolved, then pour into a bottle. This will keep in the refrigerator for up to 4 weeks.

Peppermint & Lemon Cordial

MAKES 300ML (10FL OZ)

1g (¹/₃₂oz) Rare Tea Company English Peppermint
250ml (9fl oz) hot water
250g (9oz) caster sugar
2g (¹/₁₆oz) malic acid powder

Steep the peppermint tea leaves in the measured hot water for 2 minutes. Pass through a chinois, then add the sugar and malic acid and stir until the sugar has dissolved. Leave to cool.

Once the liquid is room temperature, pour into a bottle. This will keep in a refrigerator for up to 4 weeks.

D&B Rhubarb Cordial

MAKES 800ML (27FL OZ)

500g (1lb 2oz) rhubarb, roughly chopped
500ml (18fl oz) water
250g (9oz) caster sugar
2g (¹/₁₆oz) ascorbic acid powder

Combine all the ingredients in a vacuum bag and sous-vide at 60°C (140°F) for 2 hours.

Rest in an ice bath for 15 minutes, then pass through a chinois into a bottle. This will keep in the refrigerator for up to 2 weeks.

Watermelon Cordial

MAKES 500ML (18FL OZ)

250ml (9fl oz) fresh watermelon juice
250g (9oz) sugar
5g (¹/₈oz) citric acid powder
2g (¹/₁₆oz) ascorbic acid powder

Mix the watermelon juice with the sugar until the sugar has dissolved then add the citric acid and the ascorbic acid. Pass through a chinois into a bottle. This will keep in the refrigerator for up to 4 weeks.

Rhubarb Cordial #1

MAKES 750ML (25½FL OZ)

150g (5½oz) rhubarb, sliced
250g (9oz) caster sugar
500ml (18fl oz) still mineral water
2 drops of red food colouring
5g (¹/₈oz) citric acid powder

Combine the rhubarb, sugar and measured water in a saucepan. Bring to the boil and simmer until the rhubarb has softened. Remove from the heat and leave to rest for 30 minutes.

Add the food colouring and citric acid and stir until the citric acid has dissolved. Pass through a chinois into a bottle. This will keep in the refrigerator for up to 4 weeks.

Almond Blossom Cordial

MAKES 400ML (14FL OZ)

2g (¹/₁₆oz) Rare Tea Company Rare Spanish Almond Blossom
200ml (7fl oz) hot water (100°C / 212°F)
30g (1oz) caster sugar

Steep the tea in the measured hot water for exactly 2 minutes. Strain through a paper coffee filter and leave to cool for 10 minutes.

Slowly add the liquid to the sugar, stirring until the sugar has dissolved. This cordial must be served on the day it is made.

Syrups

NOTE: As sugar syrup is so commonly used in cocktails, we have included the recipe at the front of the book (see page 21).

Heather Honey Syrup

MAKES 300ML (10FL OZ)

150g (5½oz) heather honey
150ml (5fl oz) water

Mix the honey with the measured water until the honey has completely dissolved, then pour into a bottle. This will keep in the refrigerator for up to 4 weeks.

Miso Syrup

MAKES 700ML (1¼ PINT)

200g (7oz) barley miso
400ml (14fl oz) water
2 egg whites
Caster sugar (see below)

Combine the miso and the measured water in a saucepan. Whisk the egg whites with a splash of water, then add them to the saucepan. Heat gently, stirring occasionally, until the egg white has set on the surface.

Carefully remove the egg and pass the liquid through a fine sieve and then a paper coffee filter. Weigh the strained liquid and add double the amount of caster sugar. Stir until dissolved, then pour into a bottle. This will keep in the refrigerator for up to 4 weeks.

Cane Syrup

MAKES 750ML (25½FL OZ)

250ml (9fl oz) water
500g (1lb 2oz) raw cane sugar

Combine the measured water and sugar in a saucepan over a medium heat and stir until the sugar has dissolved. Bring to the boil, then remove from the heat and pour into a bottle. This will keep in the refrigerator for up to 4 weeks.

Chestnut Honey Syrup

MAKES 600ML (20FL OZ)

400g (14oz) Rowse blossom honey
250g (9oz) fresh chestnuts
200ml (7fl oz) water

Combine the ingredients in a vacuum bag and sous-vide at 60°C (140°F) for 2 hours. Pass through a chinois into a bottle. This will keep in the refrigerator for up to 4 weeks.

Bay Leaf Syrup

MAKES 300ML (10FL OZ)

200ml (7fl oz) water
200g (7oz) caster sugar
4 bay leaves

Mix the measured water and sugar until the sugar has dissolved. Break the bay leaves into pieces, add to the syrup and leave to infuse for at least 6 hours.

Pass through a chinois into a large bottle. This will keep in the refrigerator for up to 4 weeks.

Almond Flower Syrup

MAKES 680ML (24FL OZ)

150g (5½oz) acacia honey
500ml (18fl oz) sugar syrup (see page 21)
15ml (½fl oz) Almond Blossom Tincture
15ml (½fl oz) Manuka Tincture (see page 199)
2.5ml (½ tsp) Steenbergs Natural Almond Extract
1 drop orange flower water

Mix all the ingredients, then pour into a bottle. This will keep in the refrigerator for up to 4 weeks.

Ginger Syrup

MAKES 300ML (10FL OZ)

100g (3½oz) fresh root ginger, unpeeled
200g (7oz) caster sugar

Peel the ginger and juice it. Mix the juice with the sugar until the sugar has completely dissolved.

Pass through a chinois into a bottle. This will keep in the refrigerator for up to 4 weeks.

Lapsang Souchong Syrup

MAKES 600ML (20FL OZ)

15g (½oz) loose-leaf lapsang souchong tea
200ml (7fl oz) hot water
400g (14oz) caster sugar

Steep the tea leaves in the measured hot water for 5 minutes (do not over steep or it will become tannic and bitter).

Pass through a chinois. Whisk in the sugar until completely dissolved, then pass through a chinois a second time into a bottle. This will keep in the refrigerator for up to 4 weeks.

Toasted Pineapple Syrup

MAKES 1 LITRE (1¾ PINT)

1kg (2lb 4oz) fresh pineapple slices
500ml (18fl oz) water
500g (1lb 2oz) caster sugar

Toast the pineapple slices in a deep frying pan until they begin to caramelize on both sides, taking care not to burn them. Add the measured water and sugar and bring to the boil. Remove from the heat and leave to cool.

Pass through a chinois into a large bottle. This will keep in the refrigerator for up to 4 weeks.

Cinnamon Bark Syrup

600ML (20FL OZ)

50g (1¾oz) cinnamon bark
250ml (9fl oz) hot water
500g (1lb 2oz) cane sugar

Combine the cinnamon bark and the measured hot water and leave to infuse for 30 minutes.

Pass through a paper coffee filter, then add the sugar and stir until the sugar has dissolved. Pour into a bottle. This will keep in the refrigerator for up to 4 weeks.

Rhubarb Syrup

MAKES 1.2 LITRES (2 PINTS)

350ml (12fl oz) cold-pressed rhubarb
  juice
900g (2lb) caster sugar
2g (1/16oz) ascorbic acid powder
100g (3½oz) fresh rhubarb, sliced

Combine all the ingredients in a
vacuum bag and sous-vide at 60°C
(140°F) for 3 hours.

Rest in an ice bath for 10 minutes,
then pass through a chinois
into a bottle. This will keep in the
refrigerator for up to 4 weeks.

Lemongrass Syrup

MAKES 500ML (18FL OZ)

250ml (9fl oz) water
50g (1¾oz) fresh lemongrass
250g (9oz) caster sugar

Combine the measured water and
lemongrass in a saucepan and bring
to the boil. Remove from the heat,
add the sugar and stir until the
sugar has dissolved. Leave to rest
for 2 hours.

Pass through a chinois into a bottle.
This will keep in the refrigerator for
up to 4 weeks.

Rooibos Syrup

MAKES 1 LITRE (1¾ PINT)

12.5g (½oz) loose-leaf rooibos tea
500ml (18fl oz) hot water
500g (1lb 2oz) demerara sugar

Steep the rooibos leaves in the
measured hot water for 5 minutes
(do not over steep or it will become
tannic and bitter).

Pass through a chinois. Whisk in the
sugar until completely dissolved,
then pass through a chinois a
second time into a large bottle. This
will keep in the refrigerator for up to
4 weeks.

Salted Lapsang Syrup

MAKES 500ML (18FL OZ)

10g (¼oz) loose-leaf lapsang
  souchong tea
400ml (14fl oz) hot water
50g (1¾oz) salt
800g (1lb 12oz) caster sugar

Steep the tea leaves in the measured
hot water for 10 minutes.

Pass through a chinois. Add the
salt and stir until dissolved. Add the
sugar and stir again until dissolved,
then pour into a large bottle. This
will keep in the refrigerator for up
to 4 weeks.

Purple Corn (Chicha) Syrup

MAKES 200ML (7FL OZ)

Skin from ½ a fresh pineapple
400g (14oz) dried purple corn
½ cinnamon stick
3g (1/10oz) cloves
100ml (3½fl oz) water
200g (7oz) caster sugar

Wash the pineapple skin and
combine with the remaining
ingredients, except the sugar, in a
saucepan. Bring to the boil, then
cover with foil and simmer for
45 minutes. Remove from the
heat and leave to cool.

Pass through a paper coffee
filter. Add the sugar and stir until
dissolved, then pour into a bottle.
This will keep in the refrigerator
for up to 2 weeks.

Winter Syrup

MAKES 750ML (25½FL OZ)

500ml (18fl oz) agave syrup
150g (5½oz) fresh root ginger
1 cinnamon stick
250ml (9fl oz) water

Combine all the ingredients with 125ml (4fl oz) of the measured water in a saucepan. Simmer over a low heat for 10 minutes, adding the remaining water at intervals so that the liquid is never too thick. Remove from the heat and leave to rest for 1 hour.

Pass through a chinois into a bottle. This will keep in the refrigerator for up to 4 weeks.

Black Cardamom Syrup

MAKES 500ML (18FL OZ)

6 black cardamom pods
350ml (12fl oz) hot water
750g (1lb 10oz) caster sugar

Crack the black cardamom pods and then leave to infuse in the measured hot water for 2 hours. Pass through a chinois, discarding the pods, then add the sugar and stir until dissolved.

Once the liquid is at room temperature, pour into a bottle. This will keep in the refrigerator for up to 4 weeks.

Roasted Beet Syrup

MAKES 600ML (20FL OZ)

300g (10½oz) golden beetroot, peeled and sliced
50ml (2fl oz) vodka
300ml (10fl oz) water
300g (10½oz) caster sugar

Toast the beetroot slices in a deep frying pan until they begin to caramelize on both sides, taking care not to burn them. Add the vodka and let it cook off, then add the measured water and sugar and bring to the boil. Remove from the heat and leave to cool.

Pass through a chinois into a bottle. This will keep in the refrigerator for up to 4 weeks.

Strawberry Syrup

MAKES 500ML (18FL OZ)

85g (3oz) frozen strawberries
500ml (18fl oz) cane sugar

Defrost the strawberries at room temperature.

Combine the strawberries and cane sugar in a vacuum bag. Seal and sous-vide at 52°C (126°F) for 4 hours.

Pass through a chinois into a bottle. This will keep in the refrigerator for up to 2 weeks.

Parsnip Syrup

MAKES 1 LITRE (1¾ PINT)

500g (1lb 2oz) parsnips, peeled and sliced
500ml (18fl oz) water
500g (1lb 2oz) caster sugar

Combine the parsnips and measured water in a saucepan. Bring to the boil and simmer until the parsnips have softened. Remove from the heat and leave to rest for 30 minutes.

Pass through a chinois into a bottle and add the sugar. Mix well so that the sugar dissolves completely. This will keep in the refrigerator for up to 4 weeks.

D&B Strawberry Syrup

MAKES 700ML (1¼ PINT)

700g (1lb 9oz) strawberries
700g (1lb 9oz) caster sugar

Combine the strawberries and sugar in a vacuum bag and sous-vide at 52°C (126°F) for 20 minutes.

Pass through a chinois into a bottle. This will keep in the refrigerator for up to 2 weeks.

Spicy Vanilla Honey

MAKES 500ML (18FL OZ)

200g (7oz) Rowse blossom honey
200g (7oz) Bristol Syrup Company Vanilla
150ml (5fl oz) water
40g (1½oz) Bird's Eye chillies, sliced lengthways

Wear gloves when making this syrup. Combine all the ingredients in a vacuum bag and sous-vide at 60°C (140°F) for 1 hour.

Rest in an ice bath and leave for 15 minutes, then pass through a chinois into a bottle. This will keep in the refrigerator for up to 4 weeks.

Caramel Syrup

MAKES 500ML (18FL OZ)

250g (9oz) caster sugar
250ml (9fl oz) water

Heat the sugar in a saucepan, without stirring, until it begins to brown and turn liquid. Remove from the heat and slowly add the measured water, stirring gently, until the water is fully incorporated and there are no sugar crystals. This will keep in the refrigerator for up to 2 weeks.

Café Syrup

MAKES 150ML (5FL OZ)

50g (1¾oz) white shiro miso
50ml (2fl oz) hot water
50g (1¾oz) caster sugar

Combine the miso and measured water and stir until the miso has dissolved. Slowly add the sugar and stir until dissolved, then pass through a chinois into a bottle. This will keep in the refrigerator for up to 2 weeks.

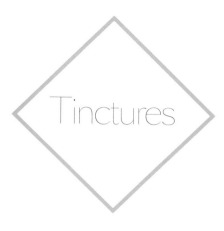

Tinctures

Roasted Almond Tincture

MAKES 250ML (9FL OZ)

**200g (7oz) blanched almonds
250ml (9fl oz) vodka**

Toast the almonds in a frying pan over a low heat until golden, taking care not to burn them. Combine with the vodka and leave to infuse for 12 hours.

Pass through a chinois into an atomizer. This will keep in the refrigerator for up to 4 weeks.

Almond Blossom Tincture

MAKES 100ML (3½FL OZ)

**2g (¹⁄₁₆oz) loose-leaf almond flower tea
100ml (3½fl oz) vodka**

Combine the tea leaves and vodka in a vacuum bag and sous-vide at 52°C (126°F) for 1 hour.

Pass through a chinois and then a paper coffee filter into an atomizer. This will keep in the refrigerator for up to 4 weeks.

Manuka Tincture

MAKES 60ML (2¼FL OZ)

**3g (¹⁄₁₀oz) loose-leaf manuka tea
60ml (2¼fl oz) vodka**

Combine the tea leaves and vodka in a vacuum bag and sous-vide at 52°C (126°F) for 1 hour.

Pass through a chinois and then a paper coffee filter into an atomizer. This will keep in the refrigerator for up to 4 weeks.

Washed

&

Infused Spirits

Atlantic Avenue Batch

MAKES 750ML (25½FL OZ)

600ml (20fl oz) Tanqueray No Ten
150ml (5fl oz) Tarragon-infused Dolin Dry Vermouth (see page 207)

Combine the gin and vermouth in a bottle. This will keep in the refrigerator for up to 4 weeks.

Banana-infused Macallan Whisky

MAKES 700ML (1¼ PINT)

100g (3½oz) dried banana
700ml (1¼ pint) Macallan Sherry Oak 12 Year Old Whisky

Combine the banana and whisky in a vacuum bag and sous-vide at 60°C (140°F) for 2 hours.

Pass through a chinois into a bottle. This will keep in the refrigerator for up to 4 weeks.

Bay leaf-infused Belvedere Vodka

MAKES 750ML (25½FL OZ)

25g (1oz) fresh bay leaves
750ml (25½fl oz) Belvedere Vodka

Combine the bay leaves and vodka in a vacuum bag and sous-vide at 65°C (149°F) for 2 hours.

Rest in an ice bath for 45 minutes, then pass through a chinois into a bottle. This will keep in the refrigerator for up to 4 weeks.

Café Espresso Batch

MAKES 300ML (10FL OZ)

250ml (9fl oz) Ketel One Vodka
160ml (5½fl oz) Mr Black Cold Brew Coffee Liqueur
25g (1oz) Fernet-Branca Menta
100g (3½oz) Valrhona Waina 35% white chocolate
100g (3½oz) banana (overripe and dark brown)
80ml (2¾fl oz) Café Syrup (see page 198)
200ml (7fl oz) milk
30ml (1fl oz) lemon juice

Combine all the ingredients, except the milk and lemon juice, in a vacuum bag and sous-vide at 60°C (140°F) for 1 hour. Remove, open the bag slightly and add the milk and lemon juice, using a funnel. Seal the bag, place in an ice bath and leave for 30–45 minutes, until the mixture starts to curdle. Pass through a paper coffee filter into a bottle. This will keep in the refrigerator for up to 6 weeks.

Barnard Batch

MAKES 260ML (9¼FL OZ)

200ml (7fl oz) The Lakes The One Fine Blended Whisky
60ml (2fl oz) Pierre Ferrand Pineau Des Charentes

Combine the whisky and Pineau des Charentes in a bottle. This will keep in the refrigerator for up to 4 weeks.

Coconut Batch

MAKES 500ML (18FL OZ)

200g (7oz) coconut oil
13g (½oz) edible rose petals
100g (3½oz) fresh lychee
500ml (18fl oz) Belvedere Vodka

Melt the coconut oil in a saucepan over a low heat until the oil has melted to a liquid, then add the rose petals, ensuring they are all covered in oil. Leave to cool, then place in a container and leave to rest for 24 hours at room temperature.

Combine the rose-infused coconut oil with the remaining ingredients in a vacuum bag and sous-vide at 60°C (140°F) for 1 hour. Place in the freezer for 24 hours, then pass through a chinois into a bottle. This will keep in the refrigerator for up to 4 weeks.

Cardamom-infused Maker's Mark Bourbon Whisky

MAKES 750ML (25½FL OZ)

750ml (25½fl oz) Maker's Mark Bourbon Whisky
4 dried cardamom leaves

Combine the whisky and cardamom leaves and leave to infuse for 24 hours at room temperature.

Pass through a chinois, discarding the leaves, then pour into a bottle. This will keep in the refrigerator for up to 4 weeks.

Coconut Butter-washed Bacardí Heritage

MAKES 700ML (1¼ PINT)

700ml (1¼ pint) Bacardí Ron Superior Heritage Limited Edition
70g (2½oz) coconut butter

Blend the rum and coconut butter, then leave to infuse for a few hours at room temperature. Put the mixture into the freezer for 24 hours. The butter will become solid and separate from the rum.

Carefully remove the layer of butter, then pass the rum through a chinois into a bottle. This will keep in the refrigerator for up to 4 weeks.

Cherry-infused Diplomático Planas Rum

MAKES 750ML (25½FL OZ)

100g (3½oz) frozen sour Fabbri Amarena cherries
750ml (25½fl oz) Diplomático Planas Rum

Defrost and drain the cherries. Combine them with the rum in a vacuum bag and sous-vide at 65°C (149°F) for 1 hour.

Rest in an ice bath for 45 minutes, breaking up the cherries in the bag to release the flavour.

Pass through a chinois into a bottle. This will keep in the refrigerator for up to 4 weeks.

Coconut-infused Campari

MAKES 700ML (1¼ PINT)

140g (5oz) coconut oil
700ml (1¼ pint) Campari

Melt the coconut oil in a saucepan over a low heat, then combine with the Campari in a sous-vide vacuum bag. Leave to infuse for 24 hours at room temperature, then refrigerate until chilled.

Pass through a chinois and a paper coffee filter into a bottle. This will keep in the refrigerator for up to 6 weeks.

Chamomile-infused Hepple Gin

MAKES 700ML (1¼ PINT)

25g (1oz) loose-leaf chamomile tea
700ml (1¼ pint) Hepple Gin

Combine the tea leaves and gin and leave to infuse for at least 8 hours at room temperature.

Pass through a chinois into a bottle. This will keep in the refrigerator for up to 4 weeks.

Coffee-infused Bitter Vermouth

MAKES 750ML (25½FL OZ)

10g (¼oz) Assembly coffee beans
750ml (25½fl oz) Martini Riserva Speciale Bitter

Combine the coffee beans and vermouth and leave to infuse for 30 minutes at room temperature.

Pass through a chinois into a bottle. This will keep in the refrigerator for up to 6 weeks.

Coffee-infused Plantation 3 Stars Rum

MAKES 750ML (25½FL OZ)

6.5g (¼oz) Ethiopian coffee beans
750ml (25½fl oz) Plantation 3 Stars Rum

Gently crack the coffee beans with a muddler, then combine with the rum. Leave to infuse for 30 minutes at room temperature.

Pass through a chinois and a paper coffee filter into a bottle. This will keep in the refrigerator for up to 4 weeks.

Fig Leaf-infused Mancino Vermouth Rosso Amaranto

MAKES 700ML (1¼ PINT)

35g (1¼oz) fig leaves, chopped
700ml (1¼ pint) Mancino Vermouth Rosso Amaranto

Combine the fig leaves and vermouth and leave to infuse for 30 minutes at room temperature.

Pass through a chinois into a bottle. This will keep in the refrigerator for up to 4 weeks.

Curry leaf-infused Mancino Secco Vermouth

MAKES 750ML (25½FL OZ)

35g (1¼oz) fresh curry leaves
750ml (25½fl oz) Mancino Vermouth Secco

Combine the curry leaves and vermouth and leave to infuse for 24 hours at room temperature.

Pass through a chinois into a bottle. This will keep in the refrigerator for up to 6 weeks.

Coffee-infused Carpano Antica Formula Vermouth

MAKES 750ML (25½FL OZ)

25g (1oz) Assembly coffee beans
750ml (25½fl oz) Carpano Antica Formula Vermouth

Combine the coffee beans and vermouth in a vacuum bag and sous-vide at 60°C (140°F) for 15 minutes.

Rest in an ice bath for 10 minutes, then pass through a chinois into a bottle. This will keep in the refrigerator for up to 4 weeks.

Douglas Fir-infused Campari

MAKES 700ML (1¼ PINT)

150g (5½oz) Douglas Fir needles
700ml (1¼ pint) Campari

Combine the pine needles and campari in a vacuum bag and leave to infuse for 1 hour at room temperature, then sous-vide at 60°C (140°F) for 1 hour.

Rest in an ice bath for 45 minutes, then pass through a chinois into a bottle. This will keep in the refrigerator for up to 6 weeks.

Green Fig-infused Michter's Bourbon

MAKES 750ML (25½FL OZ)

3 green figs, thinly sliced
750ml (25½fl oz) Michter's US*1 Kentucky Straight Bourbon Whiskey

Combine the figs and bourbon in a vacuum bag and sous-vide at 65°C (149°F) for 1 hour.

Rest in an ice bath for 45 minutes, then pass through a chinois into a bottle. This will keep in the refrigerator for up to 4 weeks.

Horseradish-infused Plymouth Gin

MAKES 750ML (25½FL OZ)

50g (1¾oz) horseradish, peeled and sliced lengthways
750ml (25½fl oz) Plymouth Gin

Combine the horseradish slices and gin in a vacuum bag and sous-vide at 65°C (149°F) for 1 hour.

Pass through a chinois and then a paper coffee filter into a bottle. This will keep in the refrigerator for up to 4 weeks.

Nashi Pear Skin Belvedere

MAKES 300ML (10FL OZ)

150g (5½oz) nashi pear skin
2g (¹⁄₁₆oz) ascorbic acid powder
300ml (10fl oz) Belvedere Vodka

Brush the pear skin with the ascorbic acid, then combine with the vodka in a vacuum bag and sous-vide at 60°C (140°F) for 2 hours.

Pass through a paper coffee filter into a bottle. This will keep in the refrigerator for up to 4 weeks.

Manuka Tea-infused Banks 5 Island Rum

MAKES 700ML (1¼ PINT)

50g (1¾oz) loose-leaf manuka tea
700ml (1¼ pint) Banks 5 Island Rum

Combine the tea leaves and rum and leave to infuse for 30 minutes at room temperature.

Pass through a chinois into a bottle. This will keep in the refrigerator for up to 6 weeks.

Gyokuro-infused Darroze 8 Year Old Armagnac

MAKES 750ML (25½FL OZ)

20g (¾oz) Gyokuro green tea leaves
750ml (25½fl oz) Darroze Les Grands Assemblages 8 Year Old Armagnac

Combine the tea leaves and Armagnac and leave to infuse for 30 minutes at room temperature.

Pass through a paper coffee filter into a bottle. This will keep in the refrigerator for up to 2 weeks.

Mandarin & Cranberry-infused Campari

MAKES 750ML (25½FL OZ)

5 mandarins
50g (1¾oz) frozen cranberries
750ml (25½fl oz) Campari

Use a microplane grater to zest the mandarins, then remove the remaining rind. Discard the rind and reserve the whole fruit. Combine the mandarin zest with 3 of the peeled mandarins, the frozen cranberries and the Campari in a vacuum bag (reserve the remaining mandarins for a garnish if using the same day). Sous-vide at 65°C (149°F) for 1 hour.

Rest in an ice bath for 45 minutes, then pass through a chinois into a bottle. This will keep in the refrigerator for up to 4 weeks.

Rooibos-infused Martini Rubino

MAKES 750ML (25½FL OZ)

2g (¹⁄₁₆oz) loose-leaf rooibos tea
750ml (25½fl oz) Martini Riserva
     Speciale Rubino

Combine the rooibos and vermouth and leave to infuse for 30 minutes at room temperature.

Pass through a chinois into a bottle. This will keep in the refrigerator for up to 4 weeks.

Saffron-infused Cocchi Americano

MAKES 500ML (18FL OZ)

2g (¹⁄₁₆oz) saffron threads
500ml (18fl oz) Cocchi Americano

Combine both the saffron and Cocchi Americano and leave to infuse for 24 hours in the refrigerator.

Pass through a paper coffee filter into a bottle. This will keep in the refrigerator for up to 4 weeks.

Poire Normandie Batch

MAKES 750ML (25½FL OZ)

270ml (9¼fl oz) Cinzano Bianco
     Vermouth
270ml (9¼fl oz) Merlet Crème de
     Poire
180ml (6½fl oz) Miclo Poire Williams
     Eau de Vie

Combine all the ingredients and pour into a bottle. This will keep in the refrigerator for up to 4 weeks.

Olive-infused Martini Ambrato

MAKES 700ML (1¼ PINT)

700ml (1¼ pint) Martini Riserva
     Speciale Ambrato
140g (5oz) green olives
2ml (½ tsp) Pectinex

Combine all the ingredients in a Thermomix, then leave to rest for 2 hours.

Pass through a chinois into a bottle. This will keep in the refrigerator for up to 4 weeks.

Milk-infused Rye Batch

MAKES 700ML (1¼ PINT)

150ml (5fl oz) milk
700m (1¼ pint) Michter's US*1 Single
     Barrel Straight Rye Whiskey

Heat the milk in a saucepan over a low heat, ensuring it does not boil. Combine the warm milk and the whiskey in a container and leave to infuse for 1 hour at room temperature – this mixture will curdle.

Pass through a chinois 3 times until the liquid runs clear, then pour into a bottle. This will keep in the refrigerator for up to 4 weeks.

Rose-infused Plymouth Gin

MAKES 700ML (1¼ PINT)

25g (1oz) edible dried rose buds
700ml (1¼ pint) Plymouth Gin

Combine the rose buds and gin in a container and leave to infuse for at least 12 hours at room temperature.

Pass through a chinois into a bottle. This will keep in the refrigerator for up to 6 weeks.

Tarragon Bitters

MAKES 200ML (7FL OZ)

30g (1oz) fresh tarragon
200ml (7fl oz) Belvedere Vodka

Combine the tarragon and vodka in a vacuum bag and leave to infuse for 3 hours at room temperature.

Pass through a chinois into a bottle. This will keep in the refrigerator for up to 4 weeks.

Nishi Batch

MAKES 750ML (25½FL OZ)

450ml (16fl oz) Nashi Pear Skin
    Belvedere (see page 204)
150ml (5fl oz) Lustau Oloroso Sherry
150ml (5fl oz) Pierre Ferrand Pineau
    Des Charentes

Combine all the ingredients and pour into a bottle. This will keep in the refrigerator for up to 4 weeks.

Rum Blend Batch

MAKES 430ML (15FL OZ)

100ml (3½fl oz) Clément Créole
    Shrubb Liqueur
300ml (10fl oz) Appleton Estate
    Signature Jamaica Rum
10ml (¼fl oz) English Harbour Rum
20ml (¾fl oz) Rhum J M XO Rum

Combine all the ingredients and pour into a bottle. This will keep in the refrigerator for up to 4 weeks.

Almond-infused Merlet Brothers Blend Cognac

MAKES 700ML (1¼ PINT)

60g (2oz) blanched almonds
700ml (1¼ pint) Merlet Brothers
    Blend Cognac

Combine the almonds and Cognac in a vacuum bag and sous-vide at 52°C (126°F) for 30 minutes.

Rest in an ice bath for 30 minutes, then pass through a chinois into a bottle. This will keep in the refrigerator for up to 4 weeks.

Vine Leaf-infused Tanqueray No Ten

MAKES 700ML (1¼ PINT)

700ml (1¼ pint) Tanqueray No Ten
25g (1oz) dried vine leaves

Combine the gin and vine leaves in a vacuum bag and leave to infuse for 2 hours at room temperature.

Pass through a paper coffee filter into a bottle. This will keep in the refrigerator for up to 4 weeks.

Cultured Butter-infused Whisky

MAKES 700ML (1¼ PINT)

100g (3½oz) The Estate Dairy
    Cultured Butter
700ml (1¼ pint) Suntory Toki Whisky

Melt the butter in a saucepan, stirring slowly, until it begins to bubble and turns golden brown. Remove from the heat, add the whisky and leave to cool.

Place the infused butter in a vacuum bag and freeze for 24 hours. Pass through a chinois into a bottle. This will keep in the refrigerator for up to 4 weeks.

Tonka Bean-infused Noilly Prat Ambré Vermouth

MAKES 750ML (25½FL OZ)

12g (½oz) tonka beans, chopped into small pieces
750ml (25½fl oz) Noilly Prat Ambré Vermouth

Combine the tonka bean pieces and vermouth and leave to infuse for 1 hour at room temperature.

Pass through a paper coffee filter into a bottle. This will keep in the refrigerator for up to 4 weeks.

Popcorn-infused Suntory Chita Whisky

MAKES 350ML (12FL OZ)

350ml (12fl oz) Suntory Chita Whisky
10g (¼oz) sweet and salty popcorn
5g (⅛oz) unsalted butter, melted

Combine all the ingredients and place in the freezer overnight.

Pass through a paper coffee filter into a bottle. This will keep in the refrigerator for up to 4 weeks.

Rooibos-infused Noilly Prat Original Dry Vermouth

MAKES 750ML (25½FL OZ)

15g (½oz) loose-leaf rooibos tea
750ml (25½fl oz) Noilly Prat Original Dry Vermouth

Combine the rooibos and vermouth in a vacuum bag and sous-vide at 60°C (140°F) for 15 minutes.

Rest in an ice bath for 10 minutes, then pass through a chinois into a bottle. This will keep in the refrigerator for up to 4 weeks.

Milk-washed Coffee Vodka

MAKES 850ML (1½ PINT)

25g (1oz) ground coffee
700ml (1¼ pint) vodka
35ml (1fl oz) Merlet C² Café & Cognac Liqueur
5ml (1 tsp) lactic acid
310ml (11fl oz) milk

Combine the ground coffee, vodka and coffee liqueur and leave to infuse for 30 minutes at room temperature.

Pass through a paper coffee filter, then add the lactic acid. Pour the alcohol into the milk (not the milk into the alcohol) and rest for 10 minutes, then strain through a paper coffee filter. If the liquid comes out cloudy, strain it again through the same coffee filter until is clear, then pour it into a bottle. This will keep in the refrigerator for up to 4 weeks.

Saffron-infused Konik's Tail Vodka

MAKES 750ML (25½FL OZ)

5g (⅛oz) saffron threads
750ml (25½fl oz) Konik's Tail Vodka

Combine the saffron and vodka and leave to infuse for 3 hours at room temperature.

Pass through a paper coffee filter into a bottle. This will keep in the refrigerator for up to 4 weeks.

Tarragon-infused Dolin Dry Vermouth

MAKES 700ML (1¼ PINT)

200g (7oz) fresh tarragon
700ml (1¼ pint) Dolin Dry Vermouth

Combine the tarragon and vermouth in a container and leave to infuse for at least 12 hours at room temperature.

Pass through a chinois into a bottle. This will keep in the refrigerator for up to 4 weeks.

Extras

Apricot Reduction

MAKES 650ML (23FL OZ)

100g (3½oz) dried apricots
250g (9oz) caster sugar
250ml (9fl oz) water
75ml (2½fl oz) Briottet Crème
    d'Abricot

Combine the apricots, sugar and water in a saucepan and simmer over a low heat. Once the sugar has dissolved, remove from the heat and leave to rest for 30 minutes.

Blitz the mixture in a blender, then add the brandy and pour into a container. This will keep in the refrigerator for up to 4 weeks.

Banana Wine

MAKES 2.5 LITRES (4½ PINTS)

1.5kg (3lb 5oz) ripe bananas, peeled
2 litres (3½ pints) fresh grape juice
440g (1lb) caster sugar
3g (¹⁄₁₀oz) Gervin GV5 White Fruit
    Wine Yeast

Blizt the bananas, sugar and grape juice in a blender. Pour into an air-locked glass jar and add the yeast. Keep at room temperature for 1 week, mixing it every day.

After 1 week, pass through a paper coffee filter into a bottle. This will keep in the refrigerator for up to 4 weeks.

Malic Acid Solution

MAKES 80ML (2¾FL OZ)

20g (¾oz) malic acid powder
80ml (2¾fl oz) water

Mix the malic acid with the measured water until the powder has completely dissolved, then pour into a dropper bottle. This will keep in the refrigerator for up to 2 weeks.

Pistachio Orgeat

MAKES 500ML (18FL OZ)

250g (9oz) unsalted raw pistachios
250ml (9fl oz) still water, plus extra to
    wash and soak
Caster sugar
2.5ml (½ tsp) orange flower water

Wash the pistachios, then cover with water and leave to soak for 2–3 hours.

Drain the pistachios, then place in a blender. Add the measured still water and blitz to a fine paste. Strain the mixture through a mesh strainer (we use a 200 Micron nut milk bag), pressing down to release the liquid.

Weigh the resulting pistachio milk, then heat gently in a saucepan. Add an equal weight of caster sugar to the pistachio milk. Remove from the heat when the sugar has dissolved and add the orange flower water. Leave to cool, then pour into a bottle. This will keep in the refrigerator for up to 4 weeks.

Oolong Tea

MAKES 700ML (1¼ PINT)

50g (1¾oz) loose-leaf oolong tea
700ml (1¼ pint) hot water

Steep the tea leaves in the measured hot water for 15 minutes.

Pass through a chinois into a bottle. This will keep in the refrigerator for up to 3 days.

Citric Acid Solution

MAKES 100ML (3½FL OZ)

20g (¾oz) citric acid powder
100ml (3½fl oz) water

Mix the citric acid with the measured water until the powder has completely dissolved, then pour into a dropper bottle. This will keep in the refrigerator for up to 2 weeks.

Saline Solution

MAKES 100ML (3½FL OZ)

10g (¼oz) salt
100ml (3½fl oz) water

Mix the salt with the measured water until the salt has completely dissolved, then pour into a dropper bottle. This will keep for up to 4 weeks.

Sweet Vermouth Blend

MAKES 750ML (25½FL OZ)

500ml (18fl oz) Martini Rosso
250ml (9fl oz) Punt e Mes Vermouth

Combine the vermouths and pour into a bottle. This will keep in the refrigerator for up to 6 weeks.

Clarified Pineapple Juice

MAKES 300ML (10FL OZ)

375ml (13½fl oz) pineapple juice
2g (¹⁄₁₆oz) agar agar

Whisk 125ml (4fl oz) of the pineapple juice with the agar agar. Pour into a saucepan and bring to a simmer for 1–2 minutes to activate the agar agar. Slowly add the remaining pineapple juice to the saucepan. Use a sugar thermometer to make sure the temperature of the juice doesn't drop below 35°C (95°F). Once the juice is incorporated, move the solution to an ice bath to set, and leave until cool.

Whisk again, then fine-strain slowly through a paper coffee filter paper into a bottle. This will keep in the refrigerator for up to 3 days.

Strawberry Sherbet

MAKES 300ML (10FL OZ)

200g (7oz) strawberries
200g (7oz) caster sugar
100ml (3½fl oz) water

Combine the strawberries and sugar in a vacuum bag and leave to infuse for 24 hours.

Add the measured water and sous-vide at 60°C (140°F) for 20 minutes.

Pass through a chinois and a paper coffee filter into a bottle. This will keep in the refrigerator for up to 4 weeks.

Grapefruit Sherbet

MAKES 500ML (18FL OZ)

175g (6 oz) yellow grapegruit rind
1kg (2lb 4oz) caster sugar
500ml (18fl oz) grapefruit juice

Microplane the grapefruit rind, then place in a bowl with the sugar. Leave to infuse for 10 minutes.

Add the grapefruit juice and stir until the sugar has dissolved. Pass through a chinois into a bottle. This will keep in the refrigerator for up to 4 weeks.

Pomelo Sherbet

MAKES 800ML (27FL OZ)

400g (14oz) caster sugar
200g (7oz) pomelo rind
400ml (14fl oz) pomelo juice

Combine the sugar and pomelo rind in a vacuum bag and leave overnight. Sous-vide at 60°C (140°F) for 15 minutes.

Rest in an ice bath for 10 minutes. Discard the rind and pour the syrup into a saucepan with the pomelo juice. Bring to the boil, then remove from the heat. Leave to cool, then pour into a large bottle. This will keep in the refrigerator for up to 4 weeks.

Lemon Sherbet

MAKES 500ML (18FL OZ)

150g (5½oz) lemon rind
200g (7oz) caster sugar
200ml (7fl oz) lemon juice
100ml (3½fl oz) water

Combine the lemon rind and sugar in a vacuum bag and leave to infuse for 24 hours.

Discard the rind. Add the lemon juice and measured water, then sous-vide at 60°C (140°F) for 20 minutes.

Rest in an ice bath for 30 minutes, then pour into a bottle. This will keep in the refrigerator for up to 4 weeks.

Smoked Saline Solution

MAKES 100ML (3½FL OZ)

2 drops of liquid smoke
20g (¾oz) table salt
80ml (2¾fl oz) water

Mix the liquid smoke and salt, then add to the measured water and stir until the salt has dissolved. Pour into a dropper bottle. This will keep for up to 2 weeks.

Vanilla Cream

MAKES 250ML (9FL OZ)

5 drops of vanilla extract
250ml (9fl oz) double cream

Mix the vanilla extract and cream until combined. This will keep in the refrigerator for up to 3 days.

Apricot Sorbet

MAKES 460ML (16¼FL OZ)

250g (9oz) Boiron apricot purée
50g (1¾oz) caster sugar
130ml (4½fl oz) water
21.25g (¾oz) glucose
2g (¹⁄₁₆oz) stabilizer
8.75g (¼oz) staboline

Combine all the ingredients in an ice cream machine and churn until frozen. This will keep in the freezer for up to 4 weeks.

Agave Caramel

MAKES 500ML (18FL OZ)

250ml (9fl oz) agave syrup
250ml (9fl oz) Monin Caramel Syrup

Mix the syrups until completely combined, then pour into a bottle. This will keep in the refrigerator for up to 4 weeks.

Nashi Pear Juice Reduction

MAKES 500ML (18FL OZ)

1kg (2lb 4oz) nashi pears
2kg (4lb 8oz) red pears
1g (¹⁄₃₂oz) ascorbic acid powder
1 tsp sea salt

Peel the pears to remove the skin. Pass the pears through a centrifugal juicer, then pass through a chinois into a saucepan. Add the ascorbic acid and sea salt. Heat for 10 minutes over a medium heat, until the liquid has reduced to approximately 500ml (18fl oz). Remove from the heat and leave to cool.

Pass through a chinois and pour into a bottle. This will keep in the refrigerator for up to 1 week.

Chamomile Tea Cold Brew

MAKES 500ML (18FL OZ)

10g (¼oz) loose-leaf chamomile tea
500ml (18fl oz) cold water

Combine the tea leaves and measured water and leave to infuse for 4 hours.

Pass through a chinois into a bottle. This will keep in the refrigerator for up to 2 weeks.

Bergamot Tea Cold Brew

MAKES 500ML (18FL OZ)

10g (¼oz) loose-leaf bergamot tea
500ml (18fl oz) cold water

Combine the the tea leaves and measured water and leave to infuse for 3 hours.

Pass through a chinois into a bottle. This will keep in the refrigerator for up to 2 weeks.

Malawi Antlers Tea

MAKES 500ML (18FL OZ)

25g (1oz) Rare Tea Company Malawi
      Antlers White Tea
500ml (18fl oz) hot water (85°C /
      185°F)

Steep the white tea in the measured
hot water for 2 minutes, then pass
through a chinois into a bottle. This
will keep in the refrigerator for up to
2 weeks.

Rooibos Tea

500ML (18FL OZ)

5g (⅛oz) Rare Tea Company South
      African Wild Rooibos
500ml (18fl oz) hot water

Steep the rooibos in the measured
hot water for 5 minutes, then pass
through a chinois into a bottle. This
will keep in the refrigerator for up to
5 days.

Vango Bitters

MAKES 100ML (3½FL OZ)

½ vanilla pod, split lengthways and
      seeds scraped
100ml (3½fl oz) Angostura bitters

Combine the vanilla seeds and
bitters and leave to infuse for 1 week.

Pass through a chinois into a bottle.
This will keep in the refrigerator for
up to 4 weeks.

Lacto-fermented Blueberry Wine

MAKES 425ML (15FL OZ)

500g (1lb 2oz) blueberries
Pinch of salt
250ml (9fl oz) verjus
120ml (4fl oz) Empirical Helena Spirit

Wash the blueberries, then combine
them with the salt in a sous-vide
vacuum bag. Seal the bag and leave
in a warm, dry place for 1 week.

Blitz the salted blueberries in a
blender with the verjus. Pass through
a chinois, add the Empirical Helena
Spirit and pour into a bottle. This
will keep in the refrigerator for up
to 4 weeks.

Pineapple Saccharum

MAKES 250ML (9FL OZ)

250g (9oz) fresh pineapple
250g (9oz) caster sugar

Combine the pineapple and sugar in
a vacuum bag and sous-vide at 60°C
(140°F) for 4 hours.

Pass through a chinois into a bottle.
This will keep in the refrigerator for
up to 4 weeks.

Apple Citrus

MAKES 500ML (18FL OZ)

500ml (18fl oz) Bramley apple juice
5ml (1 tsp) malic acid powder

Combine the apple juice and malic acid and mix until the powder has completely dissolved. Pour into a bottle. This will keep in the refrigerator for up to 3 days.

Fermented Apple

MAKES 500ML (18FL OZ)

500ml (18fl oz) cold-pressed apple juice
100g (3½oz) dextrose
0.5g (1/64oz) Gervin GV5 White Fruit Wine Yeast
1g (1/32oz) yeast nutrient

Combine all the ingredients in an air-locked glass jar. Leave to ferment at a controlled temperature (about 25°C / 77°F) for 1 week.

Pass through a paper coffee filter into a bottle. This will keep in the refrigerator for up to 4 weeks.

Japanese Ceremonial Matcha Bitters

MAKES 400ML (14FL OZ)

2g (1/16oz) Rare Tea Company Japanese Ceremonial Matcha
400ml (14fl oz) Belvedere Vodka

Combine all the ingredients in a vacuum bag and sous-vide at 52°C (126°F) for 4 minutes.

Rest in an ice bath for 15 minutes, then pass through a chinois multiple times to remove any sediment. Pour into a bottle. This will keep in the refrigerator for up to 2 weeks.

Cosmo Bitters

MAKES 200ML (7FL OZ)

100ml (3½fl oz) Pernod Absinthe
100ml (3½fl oz) Regans' Orange Bitters

Combine the absanthe and bitters and pour into a bottle. This will keep in the refrigerator for up to 4 weeks.

Chamomile-infused Blossom Honey

MAKES 700ML (1¼ PINT)

5g (1/8oz) Rare Tea Company Whole Chamomile Flowers
250ml (9fl oz) hot water (100°C/ 212°F)
500ml (18fl oz) Rowse blossom honey

Steep the chamomile flowers in the hot water for 10 minutes. Strain through a paper coffee filter.

Allow to cool for 10 minutes, then add the blossom honey and stir until dissolved. Pour into a bottle. This will keep in the refrigerator for up to 2 weeks.

Pineapple Tepache

MAKES 750ML (25½FL OZ)

5g (⅛oz) cinnamon stick
5g (⅛oz) cloves
5g (⅛oz) star anise
500ml (18fl oz) water
60g (2¼oz) gula melaka (palm sugar)
100g (3½oz) cane sugar
250g (9oz) pineapple rind
250g (9oz) fresh pineapple, cut into
    chunks
100ml (3½fl oz) pineapple juice

Toast the cinnamon, cloves and star anise in a saucepan, then add the measured water and simmer for 2 minutes – no longer, otherwise the flavour will be too intense. Add the gula melaka and cane sugar and stir until they have dissolved. Leave to simmer for 5 minutes.

Add the pineapple rind, chunks and juice, then pour into a plastic tub. Place a lid on top but not fully closed, as you want some air to get to the liquid. Leave it to ferment for 5 days at room temperature, stirring it every day.

Pass through a chinois into a bottle. This will keep in the refrigerator for up to 2 weeks.

Hot Spiced Cider

MAKES 700ML (1¼ PINT)

500ml (18fl oz) Bramley apple juice
15ml (½fl oz) fresh ginger juice
30ml (1fl oz) orange juice
16g (½oz) orange rind
2 cardamom pods
1 Ceylon cinnamon stick
2 cloves
3 star anise
1 vanilla pod, split lengthways and
    seeds scraped

Combine all the ingredients in a saucepan and bring to the boil. Simmer for 10 minutes, then remove from the heat and leave to rest for 30 minutes.

Pass through a chinois into a bottle. This will keep in the refrigerator for up to 4 weeks.

To reheat, warm slowly in a saucepan over a low heat, making sure the cider does not boil. Alternatively, sous-vide at 68°C (154°F) for 10 minutes.

Hot Chocolate

MAKES 825ML (28FL OZ)

470ml (16½fl oz) double cream
65ml (2¼fl oz) water
25g (1oz) chocolate, 55% cocoa solids
65g (2¼oz) chocolate, 70% cocoa
    solids
1 vanilla pod, split lengthways and
    seeds scraped
40g (1½oz) caster sugar
Pinch of salt

Heat the cream, the measured water, both the chocolates and the vanilla in a bowl over a saucepan filled with hot, but not boiling, water – about 85°C (185°F). This will stop the chocolate from burning. Stir constantly until melted, then pour over the remaining ingredients in a large bowl. Mix until everything is dissolved, then pass through a chinois into a bottle. This will keep in the refrigerator for up to 4 weeks.

To reheat, warm slowly in a saucepan over a low heat, making sure the hot chocolate does not boil. Alternatively, sous-vide at 68°C (154°F) for 10 minutes.

Index

The authors

DENIS BROCI

Denis, Claridge's Director of Bars, joined the team in 2008 after managing the bars at Gordon Ramsay's Maze and the Institute of Directors. He oversees the intricate day-to-day operation of running the Claridge's bars flawlessly, making sure that the desires of every single guest are singularly satisfied and that, no matter how busy we are, a regular can always be found a perch and perfectly mixed martini.

_____

I would like to thank my family – first my parents, for allowing me to follow my dreams from a very young age. My wife, Sandrine and our kids, Aiden, Matty, Emma and Adam for allowing me to do what I love.

And I would like to thank all of the past and current employees of Claridge's and its bars – your contribution has allowed us to create this book. In particular my mentor Daniel Baernreuther, who very much shaped my early development and vision when I joined Claridge's, and the senior management at Claridge's for always challenging me and trusting me with many projects over the years. Nathan McCarley-O'Neill, who has worked closely with me to ensure that every aspect of this book, from photography to recipes, development and research, has been second to none. He ensures that the new bar spaces will always offer a great experience for our guests and works closely with the teams to create an environment in which they can learn, develop, create and share their passion. Alice Taraschi and Matteo Caretta for helping us every step of the way, allowing us to try each recipe, (sometimes more than once) until we were absolutely happy with what went into this book.

It also goes without saying that this book would not have been possible without our industry peers who contributed recipes to the book. We drew so much inspiration from our research and we hope we did the drinks justice.

NATHAN MCCARLEY-O'NEILL

In 2020, Nathan was appointed Claridge's Director of Mixology from his previous role as bar director at the NoMad Hotel in New York. Nathan is driving Claridge's cocktails into the future: promoting our drinks programme around the globe, evolving new bar concepts and demonstrating that, more than 150 years after opening, Claridge's really is the quintessential London spot for a first-rate cocktail.

_____

This project would not have been possible without the support of Paddy McKillon, Paul Jackson, Jim Lyons, Paula Fitzherbert, Orla Hickey and the sensational Maybourne and Claridge's teams. Stephanie, Jonathan, Ella and the team at Octopus, your approach to perfection and understanding gave us a platform – we hope we fulfilled the opportunity you have given us. John Carey, you are a master of photography. Being able to collaborate with you and see your artistic vision was so special. I am still in awe of what we have achieved.

Denis, Alice, Matteo – we tasted over 600 cocktails, we discussed, argued and contemplated each small detail in this book. I am so proud to have worked with you.

To all our suppliers, brands, friends, colleagues, and each person that contributed to this book, I want to personally thank you. I hope we did you all proud.

Darren Leaney, you have been there since the first day we met at Milk & Honey. You are on the other side of the world but still manage every day to push to me to be better – your contribution to this book is so much greater than the drinks we included, thank you!

And finally to my wife Hana, none of this is possible without your guidance, support and love. You have given me the confidence to be able to follow what I love. Your profound influence on me is so obvious, you have taught me how to be my most genuine self, and every day I do what I do to make you proud. I love you.

Glossary

UK	US
beetroot	beet
bird's eye chilli	Thai chili pepper
blitz	blend; process
brine	salty liquid in which the ingredient is packed
calvados	a type of apple brandy
caster sugar	superfine sugar
chopping board	cutting board
cocktail skewer	cocktail pick
cordial	concentrated syrup (not the same as the US's alcoholic cordial)
coriander (fresh)	cilantro
crème d'abricot	apricot liqueur
crème de banane	banana liqueur
crème de cassis	black currant liqueur
crème de fraise des bois	strawberry liqueur
crème de mûre	blackberry liqueur
crème de pêche	peach liqueur
crème de poire	pear liqueur
dark chocolate	semisweet chocolate, or bittersweet chocolate if 60% (or more) cacao
Demerara sugar	type of raw sugar; can use turbinado or brown sugar instead
double cream	heavy cream
eau de vie	a type of fruit brandy
jug	pitcher
julep tin	julep cup
liqueur de violette	violet syrup
perry	hard cider made with pears
rocks glass/tumbler	old-fashioned glass
soda water	club soda
spirit	liquor
still (water)	noncarbonated
sugar thermometer	candy thermometer
vanilla pod	vanilla bean

Mixology notes

Standard level spoon measurements are used in all recipes:
1 tablespoon = one 15ml spoon
1 teaspoon = one 5ml spoon

Imperial and metric measurements have been given in all recipes. Use one set of measurements and not a mixture of both (see 'A note on measurements' on page 21).

All fl oz measures are imperial not US.

Always use the best, freshest ingredients. All juices should be fresh.

Milk should be full fat (whole) unless otherwise stated.

Unwaxed citrus fruits should be used for any recipe that calls for zest or peel.

To the entire Claridge's team past and present: thank you for everything you do. You are unsung heroes and without you this book wouldn't be possible.

First published in Great Britain in 2021 by Mitchell Beazley,
an imprint of Octopus Publishing Group Ltd
Carmelite House
50 Victoria Embankment
London EC4Y 0DZ
www.octopusbooks.co.uk

An Hachette UK Company
www.hachette.co.uk

ISBN 978-1-78472-800-7

A CIP catalogue record for this book is available from the British Library.

Printed and bound in Italy

10 9 8 7 6 5 4 3 2 1

Publisher: Stephanie Jackson
Creative Director: Jonathan Christie
Designer: Jeremy Tilston
Editor: Ella Parsons
Copy Editor: Sarah Reece
Contributing Editors: Frankie McCoy
    & Elle Blakeman
Research & Editing: Denis Broci &
    Nathan McCarley-O'Neill
Photographer: John Carey
Illustrator: Clym Evernden
Senior Production Manager: Peter Hunt